Maker Innovations Series

Jump start your path to discovery with the Apress Maker Innovations series! From the basics of electricity and components through to the most advanced options in robotics and Machine Learning, you'll forge a path to building ingenious hardware and controlling it with cutting-edge software. All while gaining new skills and experience with common toolsets you can take to new projects or even into a whole new career.

The Apress Maker Innovations series offers projects-based learning, while keeping theory and best processes front and center. So you get hands-on experience while also learning the terms of the trade and how entrepreneurs, inventors, and engineers think through creating and executing hardware projects. You can learn to design circuits, program AI, create IoT systems for your home or even city, and so much more!

Whether you're a beginning hobbyist or a seasoned entrepreneur working out of your basement or garage, you'll scale up your skillset to become a hardware design and engineering pro. And often using low-cost and open-source software such as the Raspberry Pi, Arduino, PIC microcontroller, and Robot Operating System (ROS). Programmers and software engineers have great opportunities to learn, too, as many projects and control environments are based in popular languages and operating systems, such as Python and Linux.

If you want to build a robot, set up a smart home, tackle assembling a weather-ready meteorology system, or create a brand-new circuit using breadboards and circuit design software, this series has all that and more! Written by creative and seasoned Makers, every book in the series tackles both tested and leading-edge approaches and technologies for bringing your visions and projects to life.

More information about this series at https://link.springer.com/bookseries/17311

Sensors and Protocols for Industry 4.0

Industrial Applications of Maker Tech

G.R. Kanagachidambaresan
Bharathi N.

Apress®

Sensors and Protocols for Industry 4.0: Industrial Applications of Maker Tech

G.R. Kanagachidambaresan
Chennai, Tamil Nadu, India

Bharathi N.
Chennai, Tamil Nadu, India

ISBN-13 (pbk): 978-1-4842-9006-4
https://doi.org/10.1007/978-1-4842-9007-1

ISBN-13 (electronic): 978-1-4842-9007-1

Managing Director, Apress Media LLC: Welmoed Spahr
Acquisitions Editor: Aaron Black
Development Editor: James Markham
Coordinating Editor: Jessika Vakili

Cover image designed by eStudioCalamar

Distributed to the book trade worldwide by Springer Science+Business Media New York, 1 New York Plaza, Suite 4600, New York, NY 10004-1562, USA. Phone 1-800-SPRINGER, fax (201) 348-4505, e-mail orders-ny@springer-sbm.com, or visit www.springeronline.com. Apress Media, LLC is a California LLC and the sole member (owner) is Springer Science + Business Media Finance Inc (SSBM Finance Inc). SSBM Finance Inc is a **Delaware** corporation.

For information on translations, please e-mail booktranslations@springernature.com; for reprint, paperback, or audio rights, please e-mail bookpermissions@springernature.com.

Apress titles may be purchased in bulk for academic, corporate, or promotional use. eBook versions and licenses are also available for most titles. For more information, reference our Print and eBook Bulk Sales web page at www.apress.com/bulk-sales.

Any source code or other supplementary material referenced by the author in this book is available to readers on GitHub (github.com/apress). For more detailed information, please visit www.apress.com/source-code.

Printed on acid-free paper

To my family, scholars, students, and dear friends.
—G.R. Kanagachidambaresan

To my family, scholars, students, and dear friends.
—Bharathi N.

Table of Contents

TABLE OF CONTENTS

TABLE OF CONTENTS

About the Authors

 **G.R. KANAGACHIDAMBARESAN** completed his PhD in information and communication engineering at Anna University, Chennai, in 2017. He received his ME degree in pervasive computing technologies from Anna University in 2012 and his BE degree in electrical and electronics engineering from Anna University in 2010.

He is currently working as a Professor in the Department of CSE at Vel Tech Rangarajan Dr. Sagunthala R&D Institute of Science and Technology. He is also a visiting professor at the University of Johannesburg. His main research interests include the Internet of Things, body sensor networks, and fault-tolerant wireless sensor networks.

He has published several reputed articles and undertaken several consultancy activities for leading MNC companies. He has also guest edited several special-issue books for Springer and has served as an editorial review board member for peer-reviewed journals. He is currently working on several government-sponsored research projects such as ISRO, DBT, and DST, and he is a TEC committee member for DBT. In addition, he is the editor-in-chief for the *Next Generation Computer and Communication Engineering* series from Wiley. He is also the managing director of Eazythings Technology Private Limited.

ABOUT THE AUTHORS

 **Dr. N. BHARATHI** works as an associate professor in the Department of Computer Science Engineering at the SRM Institute of Science and Technology in Chennai, India. She previously worked as an associate professor at the Saveetha School of Engineering, as the R&D head at Yalamanchili Manufacturing Private Limited, and as an assistant professor at SASTRA Deemed University. She works with the Internet of Things and embedded systems in addition to computer science engineering concepts.

She was awarded a PhD degree in computer science in 2014 from SASTRA Deemed University and has 18 years of work experience as an academician after working in the industrial industry on the ARM platform with the Ubuntu OS. She completed her MTech degree in advanced computing at the SASTRA Deemed University and did her MTech project internship at the Center for High Performance Embedded Systems (CHiPES) at Nanyang Technological University (NTU) in Singapore. She received her BE in computer science engineering in 2002 from the Shanmugha College of Engineering affiliated with Bharathidasan University.

She has published many research papers in reputed journals and for conferences, has written book chapters, has guided many BTech and MTech students in various domains of computer science engineering and embedded systems and is currently mentoring four research scholars. She is also a reviewer of articles for academic journals and has contributed to the AICTE-SLA project as an expert member.

About the Technical Reviewer

Massimo Nardone has more than 26 years
of experience in security, web/mobile
development, and cloud and IT architecture.
His true IT passions are security and Android.
He has been programming and teaching how
to program with Android, Perl, PHP, Java, VB,
Python, C/C++, and MySQL for more than
25 years. He has an MS degree in computing
science from the University of Salerno, Italy.
He has worked as a chief information security
officer (CISO), software engineer, chief security
architect, security executive, and OT/IoT/IIoT
security leader and architect.

Acknowledgments

Our heartfelt thanks to Apress, to Jessica Vakili, Aaron Black, James Markham, and Sowmya Thodur for helping us throughout this project, and to the executive editor, Susan McDermott. We sincerely thank the Department of BioTechnology (DBT-India) for its funding (BT/PR38273/AAQ/3/980/2020) on the smart aquaculture project.

Preface

The fourth industrial revolution is accelerating across a wide range of industries. Industry 4.0, as it's come to be known, is characterized by the integration of advanced technologies, such as the Internet of Things (IoT), artificial intelligence (AI), and big data, to create intelligent and interconnected systems that optimize industrial processes and improve productivity. Sensors, in particular, are essential components of the IoT and play a critical role in Industry 4.0 by capturing data about the physical world, including temperature, humidity, pressure, motion, and other parameters. This data is then transmitted to other devices and systems, where it is analyzed to gain insights into the performance of machines and processes. This, in turn, helps manufacturers make informed decisions about how to allocate resources in the future.

The purpose of this book is to examine how sensors, and the IoT in general, fuel Industry 4.0. This book is aimed at undergraduates as well as researchers working to develop IoT solutions for the betterment of society with the support of industry. We also delve into the ongoing transition from Industry 3.0 to 4.0.

Source Code

All the source code used in this book can be downloaded from `github.com/apress/sensors-protocols-industry4.0`.

Funding Information

Part of this book is supported by India's Department of Biotechnology (BT/PR38273/AAQ/3/980/2020).

CHAPTER 1

IIoT Supporting Technologies: Evolution, Concepts, and Challenges

"Necessity is the mother of invention" is a saying that very much applies to the evolution of technologies.

Existing technologies are constantly being improved, and new technologies are being rapidly developed. The success of a technology on the market relies on its reachability. A product needs to be accessible to a wide variety of people in different geographical regions and age groups. Users need to be exposed to the technology and then trained in a user-friendly way and for a reasonable cost. Companies that can adopt new technology quickly are the ones most likely to succeed in this ever-changing world.

This chapter covers some successful emerging technologies such as the Internet of Things (IoT), cyber physical systems, machine-to-machine communication, edge and cloud computing, digital twins, AI and machine learning, big data analytics, and the industrial Internet of Things (IIoT).

© G.R. Kanagachidambaresan, Bharathi N. 2023
G.R. Kanagachidambaresan and N. Bharathi, *Sensors and Protocols for Industry 4.0*,
Maker Innovations Series, https://doi.org/10.1007/978-1-4842-9007-1_1

Information Technology

The computer era started in the 1950s, and along with it came various peripheral and communication devices. Connectivity protocols form the basis for the flow of digital data across networks and enable people and companies to share information. Information technology (IT) plays a major role in generating information, managing it efficiently, saving it in a proper storage format, and, with the help of network resources, exchanging it between organizations when it is required. IT refers to the set of computing functionalities that can work with the evolving applications and network technologies. For hardware, it includes server machines, computers, and network components, and for software, it covers operating systems, networking software for distributed processes, and virtualization functions.

Operational Technology

Industry has evolved from a base of manual actions, machineries, automation, and intelligent industrial operations. Operational technology (OT) refers to the process of monitoring and controlling how machines work. OT covers the specific software governing industrial hardware such as machines, pipes, motors, etc. The attributes of hardware, such as heat, hydraulic pressures, etc., are monitored with industrial control systems, with specific software for data acquisition and control. OT requires humans to conduct regular maintenance and monitoring.

Nowadays, emerging technologies have led to the convergence of IT and OT to support the smooth integration of monitoring and controlling industrial machineries, and this can be performed from remote sites via the digital flow of industrial data through the Internet. The old boundary between IT and OT is erased with an emerging technology named the *Internet of Things*. The IoT communicates the information to the required remote sites to support decision-making.

Internet of Things

The IoT is a network of physical objects that has a sensing subsystem, a processing subsystem, and a communication subsystem for the purpose of monitoring, controlling, and exchanging data with servers and other devices through the Internet. The physical objects range from household consumer appliances to highly equipped industrial machineries. There are billions of connected devices, and this number is increasing rapidly every year.

The devices are connected to the Internet, and they exchange data between them. Although this seems simple, connecting all of these objects over a network in an application environment is truly a technology revolution that has changed people's lifestyles tremendously. The key components of the IoT are sensors for sensing, connectivity with the Internet, device identity for the uniqueness of a device, and actuators for controlling physical interactions. In addition, the collected data needs to be stored and processed, and the required information is retrieved for further decision-making. To enable this, the IoT devices are connected with the cloud through gateways that are responsible for transmitting the data from different sources and devices. Other possible communications are from device to device within a network, device to device beyond a network to a gateway, device to a local database, etc.

Evolution

The first IoT device was a Coke machine connected to the network in 1982 at Carnegie Mellon University. Although the origin of the IoT was projected in 1999 with the establishment of device-to-device communication, the AutoID center at MIT released many research articles on the IoT before that. In addition, LG invented an Internet-connected refrigerator with IP connectivity. The term itself was coined by Kevin Ashton, a British professor, in 1999.

From 2000 to 2008, the IoT grew gradually with devices such as Electronic Product Code from the AutoID center at MIT, single-board microcontrollers, etc. The International Telecommunication Union also published the first report to support the global acceptance of IoT technology. From 2009 onward, the growth of the IoT has been immense, eventually reaching its current status of 5G and Industry 4.0.

Challenges

There exists a number of challenges with the IoT, though the technology is helping humankind in various ways. The devices are required to be small in size, and the other limitations are connectivity, bandwidth, and lifetime. Also, the devices are more vulnerable than traditional computer machines.

Limited Connectivity and Bandwidth

The bandwidth for transmission across the Internet is generally limited for IoT devices. In addition, IoT professionals and experts are anxious that the exponential growth of the IoT will create a challenge of connectivity without an intelligent communication system.

Limited Device Lifetime

We need devices powered by batteries to be able to work continuously in all domains, particularly in the medical field. The longer the battery life of the IoT device, the higher its value in the IoT market. Manufacturers need to consider this as a key challenge, and device design must include sleep modes and the ability to operate at low voltages.

Coexistence Issue Among Devices

The usage of IoT is exponentially increasing, with 12.3 billion devices worldwide in 2021. The existence of more devices will cause distraction, noise, and interference in another device's functionality even if the signal strength is good.

Lack of Regulation

Compliance is a major concern when dealing with numerous devices with different qualities, standards, and security levels. It takes time for the government to standardize any technology, and the devices and the interfaces and protocols used for IoT are evolving rapidly.

Security

The attack surface is expanded when it comes to IoT devices, which leads to a higher chance of attackers penetrating a secured network. IoT devices are more vulnerable, which increases the potential chances of cybercriminal attacks.

Benefits

Despite many challenges, IoT devices have several advantages. IoT devices replace the variety of programmable logic controller modules, which cost more money. In addition, IoT devices provide better connectivity with the Internet for data exchange. IoT devices help manufacturers keep track of their various products, such as vehicles, biomedical machines, and industrial machinery, and help them to monitor that they are functioning properly. Additionally, the IoT enables timely servicing and avoids sudden failures. In agriculture, IoT devices can measure parameters such as temperature, humidity, soil moisture, etc., with various sensors. In addition, IoT devices can control various appliances used in homes to enable home automation.

Applications

Figure 1-1 shows some of the applications of the IoT. Smart grids can save energy with smart energy meters and sensors embedded in various devices, including energy meters. The usage of electricity is effectively monitored, and bidirectional data exchange can be useful to track power consumption. The analysis of the power consumption is used for future load predictions and thereby to plan for productivity.

IoT sensors connected to the Internet can monitor the water supply and send the data about the water flow to the cloud. The data is then analyzed to coordinate with the supply service. Any unusual change in the water flow is closely reviewed to check whether any leakage exists in the water line.

Figure 1-1. *Applications of IoT*

Wearables and smart healthcare apps help track people's health. Fitness bands, smart watches with health apps, wearable bio sensors such as gloves, ECG monitors, diabetes and blood pressure monitors, etc., are used to monitor basic health parameters. Sudden changes exceeding threshold limits cause alerts to be sent to the concerned caretakers. Logistics and supply chain systems using the IoT can save many companies time and money. More companies are undergoing a digital transformation for asset tracking with Bluetooth beacons, NFC, and RFID tags. For instance, IoT-based building construction and maintenance are necessary for safety and cost-effective construction.

Cyber Physical Systems

The term *cyber physical systems* was coined in 2006 by Helen Gill, program director for embedded and hybrid systems at the National Science Foundation in the United States. A cyber physical system is defined as an integrated system of the physical environment with the cyber world through interfaces and analog-to-digital conversions, and vice versa. Volkan Gunes et al.[1] in 2014 framed a definition of cyber physical systems in their survey about cyber physical systems by espousing the definitions of CPS experts.

They said, CPSs are "complex, multidisciplinary, physically aware next-generation engineered systems that integrate embedded computing technology (cyber part) into the physical phenomena by using transformative research approaches. This integration mainly includes observation, communication, and control aspects of the physical systems from the multidisciplinary perspective."

---

[1] Gunes, Volkan & Peter, Steffen & Givargis, Tony & Vahid, Frank. (2014). A Survey on Concepts, Applications, and Challenges in Cyber-Physical Systems. KSII Transactions on Internet and Information Systems. 8. 4242-4268. 10.3837/tiis.2014.12.001.

A CPS not only integrates the physical and computational components but also converges trending technologies such as Industry 4.0, the Internet of Things, embedded systems, machine-to-machine communication, artificial intelligence, machine learning, and fog computing.

Evolution

The ever-growing requirements in the fields of environmental science and sustainability, healthcare and medicine, manufacturing and energy industries, transportation and supply chains, smart cities, and building management systems has led to a transformation in how users interact with engineering systems. This transformation is reflected in the evolution of simple embedded systems to complex and real-time CPSs, as illustrated in Figure 1-2.

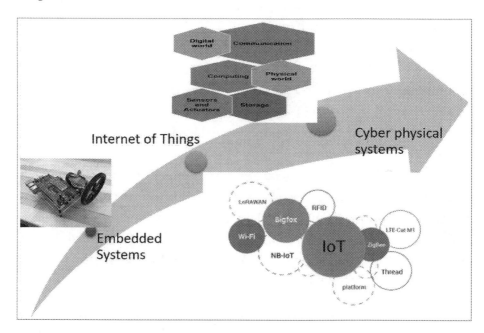

Figure 1-2. *The evolution of CPS*

Challenges

The following are the challenges:

- **Protection and security**: The data needs to be secured not only in the CPS but also in all applications. CPS is subject to more vulnerability issues, as it involves the integration of the physical and digital worlds. Those issues are addressed and resolved instantaneously.

- **Deficiency of benefit measurement**: Quantifying the benefits of the CPS is not yet standardized. The benefits should be measured specifically to an application and released on the market.

- **Industrial broadband structure**: The broadband structure also needs to be standardized to integrate physical systems with the digital world. The broadband structure in the industry highly influences the efficiency of a CPS.

- **Industrial competitors spying/disruption**: The technology market is always full of innovations. Time to market is the critical factor that almost all industries focus on with less nonrecurring engineering costs. Industry trade secrets should not be revealed to competitors to achieve success.

- **Production interruption due to data scarcity**: Generally, industrial production is highly dependent on raw materials. Currently, industries are data centric, and the exchange of information is mandatory for their continuous functioning.

Benefits

CPS paves the way for a new paradigm through its ability to interact with various industry-based applications. Sustainable development requires a concrete solution for its goals that can be achieved by adopting a CPS. A CPS also serves as one of the enabling technologies for Industry 4.0. To resolve a global challenge in smart cities, infrastructure, healthcare, etc., engineers from all disciplines from various parts of the world need to work together. Cyber physical system engineers have the potential to overcome these requirements by mastering cutting-edge technologies.

The following are the applications:

- **Independent robotics systems** consisting of physical systems are driven by cyber components. The interconnected physical components communicate with the cyber counterpart by sensing (via sensors) the environment. The cyber component processes the information received from physical components, records it, and sends feedback and control information to react to the environment through physical components (actuators), such as the direction of the next move and velocity.

- **Assistive healthcare systems** based on cyber physical systems collect all sources of inputs, such as the patient's digital report, values from sensors mounted in the patient's place or over the body, digital cameras, etc. The healthcare support system is developed with various input sources and decision-making and predictive algorithms. Hence, the CPS-based integrated monitoring and control of smart devices can assist patients in a convenient way.

- **Autonomous manufacturing systems** are the transformations of physical systems into cyber physical systems in which each component, such as machinery, automated robots, processing protocols, and the employees work together. Industry 4.0 converges the potential benefits of computers and smart devices with industrial technologies to achieve improved performance and productivity in a smarter and more effective approach.

- **Interactive traffic control systems** require the networked communication of multiple sensors mounted at the junction of roads and vehicles. The systems should manipulate and coordinate communication with vehicles as well as sensors in the road infrastructure in a time-critical manner. The correct information is exchanged properly to disseminate the traffic control information on time and trigger the actuators if required to govern the traffic. CPS-based traffic modeling systems are contributing to the development of these time-critical systems.

- **Smart power grid systems** are electric networks in which power generation, distribution, transmission, and usage are monitored and controlled in an efficient way. This enables a more sustainable and economical approach to conserving electrical energy. Large physical networks are combined with their cyber counterparts to digitize them and enable control and monitoring in an eco-friendly approach.

- **Integrated emergency response systems** are built on top of factors such as emergency management, rescue operations, warnings, and evacuation against any unexpected scenarios or disasters. Policies and protocols should be formulated and updated based on need, and forecasting the disaster, along with measures of protecting people. The combination of the physical environment with the digital world will bridge the gap and pave the way to reach the available resources when urgently needed.

Machine-to-Machine Communication

Machine-to-machine (M2) communication exchanges control and status information between devices automatically without human intervention. The large number of machines in different industries communicate with each other to cooperatively achieve the corresponding industrial process. M2M communication acts proactively based on collected data from sensors and transfers the data over the network to other parts of the industry for processing or storage. The sequence of actions is performed based on the similarity or difference or equality of the data value collected and the threshold value, if defined.

The types of M2M communication are specified based on the grouping of machines, hop-by-hop connectivity, or MAC-based connectivity. M2M communication is non-IP hardware based within a closed system. Most communication is simple for the key purpose of monitoring and control.

Evolution

The origin of machine-to-machine communication is telemetry. The telemetry period started with data communication in the Russian army in 1845, continued with two-way radio networks and telephone lines in the 1900s, and gradually evolved with innovations such as caller ID (1970), electricity power meters (1977), and single computer processing chips (1978).

The innovations of information connectivity, such as GSM, Bluetooth, and RFID, have led to next-generation technology called *machine-type communication* or *machine-to-machine communication*. At the start of the 21st century, the growth of M2M was rapid because of cellular and Internet technologies.

Challenges

The following are the challenges:

- **Limited power source**: The transmission of reasonable data to the interconnected nodes consumes power. M2M devices have almost wireless communication, power consumption is a major factor, and trade-offs exist between the volume and range of transmitting data and power consumption.

- **Lack of optimized standards**: Too many standards are available from various proprietary organizations and involved in promoting the use of their standards worldwide. An optimized standard for devices is necessary. Although it is difficult to devise an optimized standard for all domains of applications, at least domain-specific optimized standards need to be formulated.

- **Heterogeneity of devices and connectivity**: M2M devices adopt different interfacing and connectivity between devices and networks. Devices that have the same interfacing mechanisms can be connected together more easily than devices with different interfacing mechanisms.

- **Low data rate**: The amount of data needed to communicate in M2M is generally less when compared to normal communication. Since M2M has the constraint of a low data rate, limited data transmission is preferable to increase battery life. The data needs to be optimized or summarized before transmission to ensure that even at low data rates, it will reach the destined machine.

- **Node failures**: The M2M system should function despite any node failures. The handling of faulty nodes is a major concern in M2M. The data should not stagnate at the failed node. Proper alternative solutions need to be devised to recover the data from failed nodes and distribute it without any hindrance for regular functioning.

Benefits

The following are the benefits:

- Remote monitoring and proactive servicing to prevent failures and shutdown of machines

- Real-time control of devices among themselves with very little or no human intervention

- Triggers that are helpful in raising alerts and warnings automatically without the need for human resources to monitor them manually

- Tracking of products or components and keeping records of their locations to follow the path of product or component movements

Applications

The applications of M2M are ever-increasing. This section discusses a few, as illustrated in Figure 1-3.

- **Inventory administration**: Tracking raw materials or components is a tedious process, and much manual effort is needed. The inventory in any manufacturing industry can be tracked with machine-to-machine communication by monitoring the movement of components or raw materials from one unit to another.

- **Home equipment communication**: The communication between the machines inside the home and the Internet can provide a better environment autonomously without human intervention.

- **Vending machines**: Food, toys, etc., can be sold in vending machines. In the past, the products were periodically restocked by a salesperson who did not have any prior information about the stock. Currently, the machines can communicate their stock status so that it is easier for the salesperson to maintain the correct stock in the vending machine.

- **Healthcare device management**: Healthcare is one of the critical domains that requires more attention. Healthcare machines are enabled with communication mechanisms for exchanging critical or regular information to improve patient care and alert patients or doctors if any risk is occurring.

- **Utility meter control and monitoring**: The usage of resources such as water, electricity, data, etc., can be monitored. The communication between the utility meters and the control unit provides a view of the usage of resources. When complete usage details are collected and analyzed, it can increase productivity, availability, etc.

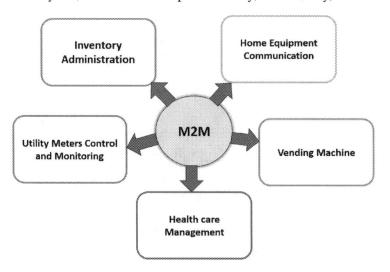

Figure 1-3. *Applications of M2M*

Edge and Cloud Computing

Cloud computing has been used for a long time and is the major technology used in almost all sectors, from healthcare to, more recently, the education sector. It transfers the data to a server located anywhere in the world that can process the data. Contrary to cloud computing, the data in edge computing is stored on nearby servers or devices. Edge computing is a change for industrial establishments to turn machine-based data into executable data using nearby resources to reduce the reaction time and receive the data rapidly using edge devices. Figure 1-4 displays the layered relationship between cloud, edge, and fog computing.

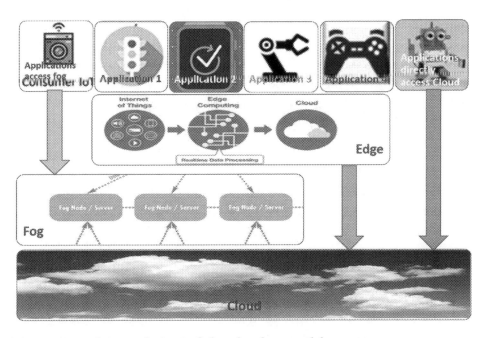

Figure 1-4. *Layered view of cloud, edge, and fog*

Evolution

The idea of cloud computing first started in 1950, when computing resources were bought for the purpose of resources in organizations, whereas edge computing evolved in the 1990s, when Akamai released a content delivery network (CDN). Edge computing is where data is collected, processed, and deployed closer to the source. Edge computing has increasingly been seen as a valuable component of industrial automation strategies. Bernard[2] notes that edge computing is not the end of cloud computing since there is no analytical framework to prove it.

---

[2] https://www.analyticsinsight.net/edge-computing-vs-cloud-computing-what-are-the-major-differences/

Challenges

Individual edge devices located in different places require several monitors to comprehend the health and status of every IT component; hence, monitoring edge devices as the number of edge devices increase is a challenge. Companies don't like to pay when there are shortages. In addition, costs rise when the number of resources starts to increase. Data storage with distributed servers must be maintained to reduce data loss due to server failures. Sensitive and private data must be secured from third-party access.

Benefits

When these challenges are overcome, the benefits can be realized. Edge computing allows crucial processing jobs to take place close to users in the deployment phase, which decreases latency. As more data flows to and from edge servers, the sum of traffic to and from central servers is decreased. The distributed nature of edge networks makes them more difficult to compromise. If a breach occurs in one area, all of the compromised sections can be addressed at the same time.

Applications

Sensors using edge computing can track nutrient density and water usage to optimize harvests and can detect real-time equipment malfunctions. In addition to electric vehicle charging stations, solar farms, and wind farms, sensors can monitor and control grid power. Edge computing is used in healthcare, manufacturing, transportation, construction, and more for processing, managing, and analyzing. It helps identify tricky data that needs instantaneous analysis to improve patient care. Manufacturing companies can utilize edge computing to improve product quality and detect production errors by incorporating machine learning and real-time analytics.

Digital Twins

A key component of the smart city hype cycle is the digital twin concept. Basically, a digital twin is a representation that functions as a digital counterpart to a physical object or process in real time. It can be considered part of robotic process automation (RPA). The benefits of digital twins are seen across many industries and sectors today, but digital twins are not widely used and are in their infancy. Learning, experimenting, and implementing digital twins are costly tasks.

Evolution

Digital twins were first applied to manufacturing by Michael Grieves of the Florida Institute of Technology. Previously, David Gelernter's 1991 book *Mirror Worlds* predicted the concept of digital twins. In an effort to improve the physical model simulation of spacecraft, NASA devised the first practical definition of a digital twin. It initially had a few different names and was later named *digital twin* by NASA scientist John Vickers.

Challenges

Despite the many benefits that the rise of this technology can bring to a company, there are more than a few challenges to overcome. It is essential for a company to have fast, reliable, and available connectivity in all the regions where it operates. The Digital Urban European Twin (DUET) project was introduced, and the goal of the DUET Digital Urban Twin project is to make digital twin technology accessible to communities of all sizes. The most difficult task is locating the necessary data to transform the digital twin into a valuable tool for all locations.

Benefits

The following are the benefits:

- The digital twin concept aims to improve the visibility and predictability of a company's assets, as well as their capacity to communicate and interact with one another.

- The digital twin can also permit business models, including those focused on servitization concepts, in which knowledge of an asset's state and effective planning of scheduled maintenance are required to provide a sufficient quality of service.

- Organizations can examine and certify a product using a digital twin before it ever existed in the real world.

- Sensors in a digital twin system generate big data in real time, allowing organizations to analyze their data and identify emerging potential system faults.

Applications

Digital twins are widely used in manufacturing, automobile, retail, smart cities, supply chain management, predictive maintenance, etc. In most corporate areas, the digital twin concept is the next big thing, as it aids in properly forecasting the future of physical assets by evaluating their digitized counterparts. Through condition monitoring and enhanced services, a digital twin helps to eliminate ambiguity during design and implementation while also enabling programs and assuring availability and reliability. By obtaining information from multiple sensing devices and intelligent technologies, the digital twin system will assist city planners and politicians in smart city development. Industrial companies that have implemented digital twins may now digitally inspect, track, and manage their systems.

AI and Machine Learning

Machine learning (ML) is a subfield of artificial intelligence (AI) that empowers systems to learn on their own with input from prior activities and experiences. There are three types of machine learning: supervised, unsupervised, and reinforcement. When an AI system undergoes *supervised learning*, it comes to a foreseeable decision based on previous data. *Unsupervised learning* is the application of AI algorithms to find data patterns with unclassified or unlabeled data points. *Semisupervised learning* is a machine learning technique that involves training using a small amount of labeled data and a large amount of unlabeled data. *Reinforcement learning* is a machine learning training strategy that rewards desirable behaviors while penalizing undesirable behaviors.

Evolution

Frank Rosenblatt invented the *perceptron*, a supervised learning technique for binary classifiers, in the late 1950s, and Christopher Watkins created the *Q-learning algorithm* in the late 1980s, which is a simple approach for agents to train how to operate in supervised conditions, which formed the basis of evolution of machine learning. Currently, machine learning is indeed steadily gaining traction in society, with real-world problems being solved by researchers' and experts' predictions and algorithms.

Challenges

In the deployment phase, businesses require machine learning tools that are simple to incorporate into their current systems. Validation of machine learning models is required to ensure that they can accurately anticipate new data. A clear explanatory ability is vital to understand "why," just as

21

it is to forecast "what" in ML problems. To maintain proper ethics, a clear process is required to understand the various biases prevalent in the ML life cycle and their possible implications.

Benefits

The communications, transportation, consumer products, and service industries have all been revolutionized by AI. Automation enables better use of raw materials, higher product quality, faster delivery, and improved security. Customers can receive highly personalized messaging from chatbots that combine conversational AI with natural language processing. Remote patient monitoring technology enables healthcare experts to promptly diagnose patients and recommend treatments without them having to seek medical treatment in person. AI can assist in ensuring that services are available 24 hours a day and that they are delivered with the same accuracy and durability throughout the day.

Applications

AI helps businesses make smart choices, and robotics can free up resources that can be put to better service. If AI is not trained to emulate human emotions, it will remain objective and assist in making the best decision possible. AI-powered chatbots can assist organizations in promptly responding to client inquiries and complaints and help in fixing disputes. Remote health monitoring technology enables clinicians and researchers to promptly diagnose patients and recommend treatments without asking them to seek medical attention in person. AI helps to track the evolution of serious illnesses and perhaps even anticipate its impacts and results.

Big Data Analytics

Data in large volumes is described as *big data*, which is built on five *V*s. The large *volume* of data is produced at a faster rate and with ever-increasing *velocity* to match real-time systems. In addition, the data is generated from different sources, such as data from mobile phones, sensors, surveys, and cloud applications. A *variety* of data is generated with different importance to the business. Among the diverse nature of data, the *veracity* refers to the quality of data and how useful it is for business and decision-making. Above all, the worthiness of the data is directly proportional to the *value* of the business in the data market.

Evolution

The growth rate of information was predicted in 1944 as an *information explosion* by Fremont Rider (big data stage 1). The need for storage capacity was envisioned, and technologies such as data mining, data warehousing, and statistical analysis emerged along with the structured content of DBMSs/RDBMSs (big data stage 2). The advent of web-based information retrieval and analysis, such as social media and online surveys, then came along (gig data stage 3). Mobile-based and sensor-based data collection and decision-making along with data visualization make up the current scenario where actual big data processing is performed using technologies such as Hadoop, Spark, Hive, QlikView, and Tableau (big data stage 4).

Challenges

It's a challenge to understand big data with all the diverse technologies needed to work with the voluminous amount generated more quickly than ever before. The data can be unstructured, semistructured, or structured and needs to be integrated to make it useful for further processing, such as decision-making and data visualization. Handling data requires a well-trained professional such as a data scientist or data engineer. The tools and technologies for handling data are evolving at a fast rate, so experts need to stay up-to-date. Moreover, securing data is a major concern and a common challenge in all domains.

Benefits

The following are the benefits:

- Streaming analytics are used to perform real-time computational analysis on live data generated continuously.

- Supply chain analytics is highly useful in decision-making based on the data generated in the process of transforming raw material to end products in industries.

- Predictive analytics helps in predicting the near future based on the available data sets and machine learning and statistical models.

- Diagnostic analytics is a process to identify the key cause of any deviation in regular activities along with the reason behind it.

- Prescriptive analytics explores the possible outcomes using machine learning and AI techniques. It recommends the path to follow based on the simulations and models developed and analyzed.

Applications

Customer relationship management is built around big data based on interactions with customers and their feedback about products on the Web, such as social media and blogs.

The perceptions of customers about a company's brand and the company itself can be improved with big data analysis. In addition, recommendation engines can suggest the products that are frequently bought by other customers and offer them during purchases.

Market basket analysis is used to improve the sales of various products and to study product sales patterns.

The maintenance of machines and components in industries is carried out to avoid failures; preventive maintenance analytics are also possible.

Big data plays a critical role in healthcare; each patient can be treated for their disease based on the genealogical origin of their illness.

Industry 4.0

Industry 4.0 refers to the data-driven revolution of production in a linked world of big data, people, processes, services, systems, and IoT-enabled industrial resources. It combines physical production and operations with smart digital technology, machine learning, and big data to create a more holistic and linked environment for production and logistics management. It enables corporate leaders to have a better understanding of and control over every area of their operations; it also allows them to use real-time data to raise efficiency, streamline processes, and drive growth.

Evolution

Since the start of the industrial revolution in the 18th century, modern industry has made significant progress. With the arrival of water- and steam-powered machines and the first weaving loom in 1784, Industry1.0

created an industry-focused culture that centered equally on quality, efficiency, and scale. The second industrial revolution began in the 20th century (Industry 2.0). The introduction of electrically powered machinery was a major factor in this breakthrough. Advancements in the electronics sector sparked the next industrial revolution, which resulted in Industry 3.0. In the 1990s, the Internet and telecommunications industry boomed, causing structural shifts in manufacturing and resulting in Industry 4.0.

Challenges

With the digital revolution, there has been an increase in concerns about data and IP privacy, ownership, and management. Corporations' proprietary data systems and processes are insufficient to facilitate cross-organizational data exchange. Companies' capacity to innovate is hampered by their inability to simply "swap out" one vendor for another or one portion of the platform for another because of a lack of interoperability. Application framework flaws as well as hardware functional flaws must be anticipated by businesses. Since more businesses rely on AI, organizations will be confronted with more data that is produced at a quicker rate and expressed in a variety of formats. AI algorithms must be easy to understand to sift through this kind of big data. All the foregoing difficulties must be addressed as quickly as possible if you are to compete and even survive in today's world.

Benefits

Enhanced production and productivity, enhanced flexibility and agility, and increased profitability are all advantages of Industry 4.0, which also enhances the user experience. Advances in technology, such as digital transformation, will assist employers in becoming smarter and more efficient in the long run. Industry 4.0 technologies allow you to gain a better understanding of your manufacturing process, supply chains, distribution systems, business outcomes, and products. You can also generate greater, better, and perhaps more inventive products with them. Industry 4.0 is designed to help you respond to consumer changes more quickly than your competitors. You will save money overall by making the best use of resources, reducing waste, improving quality, and reducing downtime.

Applications

Healthcare has benefited greatly as a result of the Industrial Internet of Things, big data, cloud computing, and AI. Industry 4.0 has played a significant role in healthcare, as it has reduced time and costs and enables the implementation of better solutions. Perhaps some of the most notable developments include IoT-based remote monitoring systems, cloud-based record systems, and quick connectivity. Smart factories will be able to enhance their efficiency to previously unthinkable levels thanks to improved efficiency and capability for continual development.

Summary

This chapter covered various technologies, such as Internet of Things, cyber physical systems, machine-to-machine communication, edge and cloud computing, digital twins, AI and machine learning, big data analytics, and Industry 4.0. We discussed the evolution of each technology, the concepts behind them, the general benefits, and their applications to provide better insights about the role of Industrial IoT.

CHAPTER 2

Sensors for the Industrial Internet of Things

Sensors are part of our day-to-day life. They monitor the environment as well as people in places such as offices, hospitals, shops, and the home. They also are in trains, planes, and cars; machines such as vending machines and ATMs; home appliances such as washing machines and refrigerators; and factories. They can be used to monitor changes such as temperature humidity, pressure, and more.

Specifically, a *sensor* is a device that receives a signal from its environment as input. The signal can be in the form of an electrical pulse, heat, light energy, or a chemical reaction. After receiving the signal, the sensor converts it into its digital representation. Digital output is fed into the processing unit, and the necessary action or response is triggered with respect to the received output.

In this chapter, you will learn how smart sensors work, features of smart sensors required for the Industrial IoT (IIoT), basic types of smart sensors, various sensors in each category and their specifications, and applications of each type of sensor.

© G.R. Kanagachidambaresan, Bharathi N. 2023
G.R. Kanagachidambaresan and N. Bharathi, *Sensors and Protocols for Industry 4.0*,
Maker Innovations Series, https://doi.org/10.1007/978-1-4842-9007-1_2

Introduction to Smart Sensors

Smart sensors measure physical environments around us. They can collect data accurately with no errors or noise. They are generally used for critical scientific applications, highly secured systems, smart grids, and more. A smart sensor consists of an embedded processor and a communication module to monitor and maintain the various subsystems and communicate the deviations or a summary to the master microprocessor. In addition, very large-scale integration technology (VLSI) and micro-electro mechanical systems (MEMSs) may be included if required to manipulate large data in less than a second. The configuration submodule in a smart sensor is also used to detect installation and placement errors.

Figure 2-1 shows the functionalities of smart sensors.

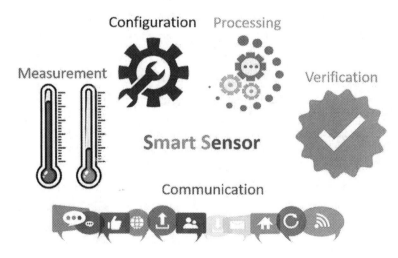

Figure 2-1. *Functionalities of a smart sensor*

The processing unit governs the computation, conversion, digital processing of data, and so on. It also decides on the amount of data to be stored in the local memory. The verification submodule verifies the correctness of smart sensors for repeatability, accuracy, reliability, etc.

Smart Sensors and the IIoT

The IIoT employs smart sensors to monitor the progress of machines. The following features are the basic requirements for a smart sensor to be installed in machines of industries:

- **Low cost, small size, and low power consumption**: Sensors can be installed in large numbers if it is economical. They are almost negligible in size and have a longer lifetime if power consumption is low.

- **Wireless communication**: Data needs to be communicated through a wireless connection with the master or to the cloud so as to update the status of the machines or attached devices. A wired connection is not suitable for sensors and IIoT.

- **Robustness**: The sensor must be able to withstand the various environmental conditions and physical contacts with other components in the environment.

- **Autonomic**: The sensor should be capable of configuring its deployment, initializing its attributes to start sensing, validating its sensing values, detecting its errors if any, repairing its own errors, and more. In other words, sensors need to be self-configuring, self-calibrating, self-validating, self-diagnostic, and self-healing.

- **Local preprocessing**: It is not necessary for each piece of data the sensor is sensing to be transmitted to the master or cloud. Local processing helps to summarize data and therefore reduce the amount of data transferred to the master or cloud.

Information that is collected from multiple sensors can be combined to monitor the overall performance of the system and any maintenance requirements. The term *soft sensors* is used when more than one physical sensor's output is combined through software. The purpose is to optimize the utilization of the industrial machines and improve the overall performance.

There are various types of IIoT sensors, as listed in Figure 2-2, although few IIoT sensors suit almost every industry. The main role of IIoT sensors is to monitor the safety of components any abnormalities. For example, temperature and humidity sensors help to prevent material or product spoilage and save machines from danger due to overheating. Pressure sensors have an alarm if there is too much pressure that will damage the machine.

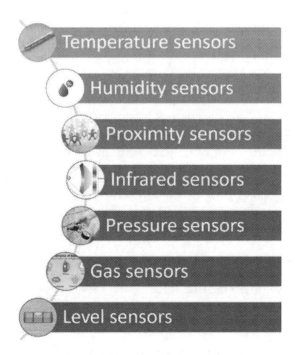

Figure 2-2. *Common sensors for the IIoT*

The proximity of industry components needs to be monitored to prevent collision; this is what proximity sensors monitor. Infrared sensors are useful in detecting the presence of any other living being. Gas sensors help to prevent leakage and safeguard human resources from dangerous situations. Level sensors are helpful in ensuring the efficient flow of oils or any liquids. The following sections discuss each type.

Temperature Sensors

The device that measures the temperature of the environment and converts the input signal to digital data is known as a *temperature sensor*. There are various types of temperature sensors categorized based on the requirement of direct contact with an object whose temperature is to be monitored. There are contact temperature sensors and noncontact temperature sensors.

MAX31820MCR+

Figure 2-3 shows the MAX31820MCR+ sensor manufactured by Maxim Integrated, which provides 9-bit to 12-bit temperature data. It communicates over one wire bus with only one data line. The other two pins are for ground and optional power supply.

Figure 2-3. *MAX31820MCR+ temperature sensor*

MAX31820MCR+T

Figure 2-4 shows the MAX31820MCR+T sensor manufactured by Maxim Integrated, which provides 9-bit to 12-bit temperature data. It belongs to the same family as MAX31820. In MAX31820MCR+T has straight leads available in bulk packs, whereas a formed lead is available as tape and in reel packs (which is why it has a *T* in its name).

Figure 2-4. *MAX31820MCR+T temperature sensor*

MAX7501MSA+

Temperature is measured more accurately with the temperature sensor MAX7501MSA+, which belongs to the MAX7500-MAX7504 family of Maxim Integrated. Figure 2-5 shows the MAX7501MSA+ sensor, which is an 8-pin IC. The input signal is communicated through an I2C-compatible, serial interface. Serial data and serial clock are the two wires in serial communication with ground, power supply, overtemperature shutdown (OS) output, three-pin address input, and reset active low input. The OS pin is used for detecting overtemperature and can raise an alarm or force an interrupt or shutdown.

Figure 2-5. *MAX7501MSA+ temperature sensor*

MAX6613MXK+T

The five-pin SC70 package low-precision analog output sensor belongs
to the MAX6613 family, as shown in Figure 2-6. This sensor is well suited
for portable devices in which optimized battery usage is necessary. Unlike
the previous sensors, the analog output voltage is proportional to sensing
temperature by this sensor. Among the five pins, two are connected
to ground (pins 2 and 5), one can be left unconnected (pin 1), one is
connected with the supply voltage (pin 4), and one is output as voltage
(pin 3).

Figure 2-6. *MAX6613MXK+T temperature sensor*

MAX31730ATC+

The MAX31730 temperature sensor is a three-channel remote temperature sensor with one local and three remote channels. It also addressable with eight slave addresses and can be connected through I2C or SMBus interfaces to microcontrollers. The two-wire interface follows SMBus protocols to configure the threshold temperatures as well as read temperature data. This sensor is available in a 10-pin μMax or 12-pin TDFN with an exposed pad, as shown in Figure 2-7.

Figure 2-7. *MAX31730ATC+ temperature sensor*

DS18B20 Waterproof Digital Temperature Sensor

The temperature of an object inside any water reservoir can be measured using the DS18B20 waterproof digital temperature sensor, as shown in Figure 2-8. The stainless-steel tube that is 6mm in diameter and 30mm long encapsulates the sensor to prevent it from rust. It provides 9-bit to 12-bit digital data with one wire interface, ground, and optional power supply. Every sensor holds a 64-bit code as its ID to uniquely identify it when more than one sensor is connected along the same wire. This sensor has an alarm system when the temperature exceeds the threshold of 750ms as its response time.

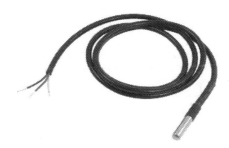

Figure 2-8. *DS18B20 temperature sensor*
Source: https://robu.in/wp-content/uploads/2017/09/sensor-de-temperatura-ds18b20-prova-d-agua.jpg

Temperature Sensor Specifications

Table 2-1 shows the specifications of the discussed temperature sensors and their operating temperature range in Fahrenheit.

Table 2-1. *Specifications of Temperature Sensors*

Temperature Sensor	Operating Temperature Range in Fahrenheit
MAX31820MCR+	131 to 257 Fahrenheit
MAX31820MCR+T	131 to 257 Fahrenheit
MAX7501MSA+	131 to 257 Fahrenheit
MAX6613MXK+T	131 to 266 Fahrenheit
MAX31730ATC+	147.2 to 302 Fahrenheit
DS18B20 Waterproof Digital Temperature Sensor	131 to 257 Fahrenheit

Applications

The following are the applications of this type of sensor:

- Temperature monitoring systems inside buildings, equipment, or machinery

- Thermostatic controls and thermometers

- Medical instruments

- Cellular phones

- Measuring temperatures in wet environments

Humidity Sensors

A humidity sensor, or *hygrometer*, reads the moisture and temperature of air, closed spaces, or soil. The relative humidity is measured as a ratio of moisture in the atmosphere to its full capacity at a specific temperature. It is most useful in comfort-based applications such as heating, ventilation, and air conditioning (HVAC) in smart public buildings. The combination of output of humidity sensors with other sensors enhances the intelligence of IIoT applications. Some of the performance measures of humidity sensors are accuracy, response time, robustness, etc., which in turn affect the cost of the sensors and their application.

Honeywell Humidity Sensor HIH-4000-003

There are various humidity sensors on the market. Let's start by looking at the Honeywell humidity sensor HIH-4000-003, which you can see in Figure 2-9.

Figure 2-9. *HIH-4000-003 humidity sensor*

The HIH-4000 family of humidity sensors is designed for high-volume original equipment manufacturers. The sensors are available in three-pin packages with one supply voltage, voltage output, and ground, as shown in Figure 2-9. An 80kohm resister needs to be connected between the voltage output and ground when connected with microcontrollers. The sensor is a laser-trimmed sensing element with on-chip signal conditioning and offers the best resistance from hazards such as dust, wet, etc. The sensor is sensitive to light and generally shielded to avoid bright lights to get better performance.

DHT11 Temperature and Humidity Sensor

The DHT 11 sensor combines temperature and humidity measurement with a digital module capturing both features. It is available in two forms, a sensor as well as a module. The sensor comes in four-pin packages, whereas the module form comes with three-pin packages, as shown in Figure 2-10. The difference is the module form has a filtering capacitor and a pull-up resistor built in. This sensor supports high reliability and lasting stability.

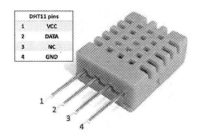

Figure 2-10. *DHT11 humidity sensor*
Source: $https://robu.in/wp-content/uploads/2016/05/51-fjA52JRL._SX355_.jpg$

Soil Humidity Sensor

The moisture of the soil can be measured using a soil moisture sensor by just inserting it into the soil. This type of sensor features dual output, for both digital and analog data. If the sensor output is more than the threshold, an LED indicator is triggered to the ON state. The digital output provides the moisture level of the soil. It has four pins: ground, supply voltage (3.3V to 5V), digital output connector, and analog output connector, as shown in Figure 2-11.

Figure 2-11. *Soil humidity sensor*
Source: $https://robu.in/wp-content/uploads/2016/03/12251.jpg$

DHT22 Sensor

The DHT22 measures temperature and humidity using a capacitive sensor and thermistor. The signal sensed is sent as digital data out through pin 2. Pin 1 is the power supply, pin 4 is ground, and pin 3 is no connection, as shown in Figure 2-12. When the master microcontroller transfers the start signal, the mode of DHT22 changes from low-power consumption mode to execution mode and starts sending 40-bit data, which includes 8-bit integral relative humidity, 8-bit relative humidity in decimal, 8-bit integral temperature, 8-bit temperature in decimal, and finally 8-bit checksum for error detection. The constraint in sensing for the DHT22 is a 0.5 sampling rate; in other words, it measures once every two seconds.

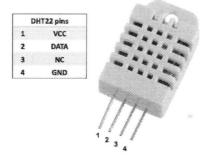

Figure 2-12. *DHT22 humidity sensor*
Source: https://robu.in/wp-content/uploads/2018/12/
DHT22AM2302-Digital-Temperature-Humidity-Sensor-4.jpg

Humidity Sensor Specifications

Table 2-2 lists the specifications of the humidity sensors.

Table 2-2. *Specifications of Humidity Sensors*

Humidity Sensor	Humidity Range
Honeywell humidity sensor	0–100%
DHT11 humidity sensor	−20 to +60°C
Soil humidity sensor	5 to 95% RH
DHT22 sensor	ADC value from 0 to 1023

Applications

The following are the applications of this type of sensor:

- Refrigeration equipment

- HVAC

- Weather station and humidity regulator

- Gardening

- Irrigation systems

- IoT temperature monitoring system

- Medical devices

Proximity Sensors

Proximity sensors are used to detect objects without physical contacts. These sensors possess a longer lifetime than others because they have no mechanical parts or physical contact. The basic working principle of proximity sensors is to sense the return signal or reflect a signal to detect objects. The objects detected by these types of sensors are called *targets*. The various types of proximity sensors are optical (light or infrared), inductive, capacitive, magnetic, and ultrasonic.

Infrared Light Proximity Sensors

Let's run through the various proximity sensors available on the market, beginning with infrared, tube-type inductive, RS PRO Capacitive barrel-style, and ultrasonic distance proximity sensors. The infrared (IR) proximity sensor depicted in Figure 2-13 has three pins similar to other sensors: power supply, ground, and output data.

Figure 2-13. *Infrared light proximity sensor*
Source: *https://robu.in/wp-content/uploads/2016/01/IR-sensor-Module-2.jpg*

The IR transmitter LED emits the light in IR frequency. The light passes on the object, if any, in front of the sensor and reflects to the sensor. The sensor has a photo diode that receives the reflected signal and converts it into voltage with a series resistor based on the intensity of light reflected. The voltage drops at the series resistor, and the threshold voltage calibrated is compared using opamp. The LED at the opamp output turns on if the voltage drop is higher. The resistor used is preset and can be adjusted to detect an object at various distances.

E18-D80NK IR Proximity Sensor (PNP)

This PNP type proximity sensor is small in size, is inexpensive, and has three wires to connect: ground, power supply, and digital output (as shown in Figure 2-14). The detection range of distance is 3cm to 80cm. It has an assembly of lens and potentiometer built in to set the range. If an obstacle or object exists, the switching signal will be high, and if no object exists, the signal remains low. Also, its power consumption is less than others.

Figure 2-14. *E18-D80NK infrared PNP-type proximity sensor Source: https://robu.in/wp-content/uploads/2015/08/ art_42009850.jpg*

Tube-Type Inductive Proximity Sensor

This sensor is of NPN type and contactless. When any metal object approaches the sensor, an Eddy current is produced in the metal, which fluctuates the magnetic field generated by the sensor. Without any spark or pressure, a signal is generated. If the change in the magnetic field is sensed beyond the threshold, the object is detected. These sensors are easy to deploy and robust in extreme environments. The interfacing can be performed by connecting the ground, power supply, and output signal, as shown in Figure 2-15.

Figure 2-15. *Inductive proximity sensor*
Source: https://robu.in/wp-content/uploads/2017/09/410w
RFhHXL._SX342_.jpg

RS PRO Capacitive Barrel-Style Proximity Sensor

The sensors are capable of detecting metal and nonmetal things. The working principle of this sensor is based the electrical signal by which the capacitance value will change. The change in the capacitance happens due to the change in the electrical field around the sensor when the objects move. As with other sensors, it has three pins, as depicted in Figure 2-16. This sensor is particularly useful in industries where attributes such as pressure, thickness, and liquid levels are needed to measure in an integrated way.

Figure 2-16. *Capacitive proximity sensor*

Ultrasonic Distance Sensor

Ultrasonic sensors are highly used sensors that detect objects, even powders. These sensors are connected to the master microcontroller with four pins, as shown in Figure 2-17. They are power supply, ground, trigger as input to initiate the emission of ultrasonic waves, and echo as output, which goes high for the duration of the wave returning to the sensor. This sensor can withstand dirt and harsh environments, reliably works well in transparent environments, and detects objects with changing colors.

Figure 2-17. *Ultrasonic proximity sensor*
Source: *https://robu.in/wp-content/uploads/2014/08/download.jpg*

Proximity Sensor Specifications

Table 2-3 lists the detecting distances for each proximity sensor discussed.

Table 2-3. *Specifications of Proximity Sensors*

Proximity Sensor	Detection Distance
IR proximity sensor	2cm to 30cm
E18-D80NK IR proximity sensor	3cm to 80cm
Tube type inductive proximity sensor	5mm to 50mm
RS PRO capacitive barrel-style proximity sensor	15mm
Ultrasonic distance sensor	2cm to 400cm

Applications

The following are the applications of this type of sensor:

- Smartphones

- Parking spaces

- Robots to avoid obstacles

- Industrial assembly lines

- Detecting a variety of metals

- Precise positioning of molds

- Level sensing in production

- Robotic projects

Infrared Sensors

Infrared sensors work based on infrared light, with the wavelength ranging from 780nm to 50μm. IR sensors help to detect motion in a well-defined angle range. They detect infrared light radiation, which changes over time when people move. There are two major types of infrared sensors. One is an active infrared sensor, which emits IR radiation and measures the reflection back to the receiver of the sensor. Another type is a passive infrared (PIR) sensor, which does not emit any IR radiation but receives it from objects that naturally emit it.

Infrared Obstacle Avoidance Sensor

This sensor is available as an assembled module with four pins to the interface, as shown in Figure 2-18. Power supply, ground, output, and enable (EN) are connected to avoid obstacles. The enable pin is used to control the sensor even through an external source with a jumper. Two potentiometers exist in the assembled module, one for managing the operating frequency and the other to control intensity. The sensor works well with smooth white surfaces rather than hard black surfaces.

Figure 2-18. *Obstacle avoidance IR sensor*
Source: *https://robu.in/wp-content/uploads/2019/04/
Infrared-Obstacle-Avoidance-Sensor-Module.png*

ISB-TS45D Infrared Thermopile Sensor

This sensor is designed for contactless temperature measurement. The working principle behind this sensor is to convert heat thermal energy into electrical voltage. In addition, these sensors are specifically for indoor usage and can be used outdoors with suitable moisture proof and optical filters. There are four pins, as shown in Figure 2-19, in which two pins are for thermophile itself as + and -, one pin needs to connect with ground, and pin 4 is for thermistor. The higher the temperature, the more infrared energy that is produced.

Figure 2-19. *ISB-TS45D thermopile sensor*
Source: `https://robu.in/wp-content/uploads/2020/09/infrared-`
`thermopile-sensor-isb-ts45d.jpg`

TCRT5000: Reflective Infrared Optical Sensor

The reflective IR optical sensor transmits the IR light, and the reflected
light is observed by its phototransistor. The amount of light reflected on
the phototransistor influences the current flow collector-emitter junction.
It has four pins: power supply, ground, digital output, and analog output
(as shown in Figure 2-20). At the analog output, the voltage is varied as
the infrared light it receives varies. At the digital output, if the amount of
infrared light is high, the output is low, and vice versa, based on the trigger
value configured at the potentiometer.

Figure 2-20. *TCRT5000, reflective infrared optical sensor*
Source: https://robu.in/wp-content/uploads/2017/06/
Elecrow-10pcs-lot-TCRT5000-Reflective-Infrared-Sensor-
Photoelectric-Switches-TCRT5000L-Sensor-Module-Kit.jpg

HC-SR505 Mini Infrared PIR Motion Sensor Infrared Detector Module

This sensor is known as a mini passive infrared motion sensor; it consumes less power and is more suitable for battery-powered applications. The sensor senses the moving object within its detecting area by changing its IR radiation and issues a high signal at the output. If no motion is detected, the output stays low. Hence, if the environment is static, the output is always low. The three pins are ground, power supply, and output, as shown in Figure 2-21.

Figure 2-21. *HC-SR505 IR detector module*
Source: `https://robu.in/wp-content/uploads/2017/04/1pcs-`
`HC-SR505-font-b-Mini-b-font-Infrared-font-b-PIR-b-font-`
`Motion-font.jpg`

Raspberry PI Infrared IR Night Vision Surveillance Camera Module

The Raspberry Pi IR camera was developed for night vision and can be used for surveillance and for studying the behavior of nocturnal insects or animals. The camera interfaces with the master processor through a camera serial interface (CSI) defined by the Mobile Industry Processor Interface Alliance. The 5-megapixel camera module captures very clear photos and videos too. The camera is connected with the Raspberry Pi board via a CSI slot on the upper surface. Since this port is for multimedia, the data rates are higher and carry only pixel data. It has a flexible ribbon cable, as shown in Figure 2-22, which can be turned to any direction while installing.

Figure 2-22. *Raspberry Pi IR camera*
Source: `https://robu.in/wp-content/uploads/2017/12/New9.jpg`

It is an IR proximity sensor, but since it is using infrared light as its source to detect the target, it is categorized under infrared sensors also.

Infrared Sensor Specifications

Table 2-4 depicts the specifications of infrared sensors with detection distance and detection angle.

Table 2-4. *Specifications of Infrared Sensors*

Infrared Sensor	Detection Distance	Detection Angle
Infrared obstacle avoidance sensor	2cm to 40cm	35 degrees
Infrared thermopile sensor	1.125×1.125 mm	90 degrees
Reflective infrared optical sensor	1.5cm	
HC-SR505 mini infrared pir motion	3 meters	100 degrees
Infrared IR night vision surveillance camera		3.6mm (focal length)
IR sensor	2cm to 10cm	35 degrees

Applications

The following are the applications of this type of sensor:

- Obstacle avoidance car assembly line count

- Robot obstacle avoidance

- Noncontact temperature measurement ear thermometer, forehead thermometer

- Line-tracking robots

- Body induction lamps, body sensors, toys
- Video surveillance system

Pressure Sensors

The sensors that have a pressure-sensitive element as their component to measure the pressure applied on them are called *pressure sensors*. There are various working principles to detect the pressure applied to the sensors. Capacitive pressure sensors employ a variable capacitor with a diaphragm to detect the amount of pressure applied in the cavity to change its capacitance value. The capacitance value is then converted to output. Resonant pressure sensors detect the pressure based on the change in the resonant frequency of the resonating component. Strain gauge-based sensors are equipped with metal strain gauges on which the pressure is applied. Piezo resistive sensors consist of a diaphragm with integrated gauges to detect the pressure applied.

BMP180 Digital Pressure Sensor

The BMP-180 sensor measures the barometric pressure, temperature, and altitude where it is mounted. There are five pins. Two pins are used for the I2C interface so it can communicate the measured parameter. The other pins are 5V power supply, 3.3V power supply, and ground, as shown in Figure 2-23. This sensor is also available in a four-pin design without a 3.3V pin. This sensor is robust to EMC with high accuracy.

Figure 2-23. *BMP180 digital pressure sensor*
Source: https://robu.in/wp-content/uploads/2020/10/BMP180-
Digital-Barometric-Pressure-Sensor-Module.png

Pressure Transmitter Sensor

Pressure transmitters, as depicted in Figure 2-24, are used mainly in
industry to measure pressure in gas, oil, air, etc. They can measure
absolute, gauge, or differential pressures. The mechanical pressure is
converted into an analog electrical signal by the sensor. The pressure
on the sensor is transmitted to the diaphragm; it either compresses or
expands, which in turn changes the resistance value. If the change goes
beyond the threshold, an alarm is raised.

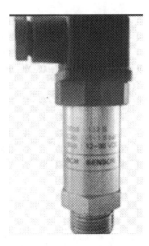

Figure 2-24. *Pressure transmitter sensor*

Honeywell HSCSAAN010ND2A3 Pressure Sensor

The high accuracy silicon ceramic (HSC) series sensors are board-mounted pressure sensors. They are calibrated in the temperature range between 32°F to 122°F and operate with either 3.3V or 5V. These sensors also measure gage, differential, and absolute pressures. The differential version compares two different pressures; the absolute version measures the pressure in vacuum, and the gage version measures the atmospheric pressure. The sensor is shown in Figure 2-25. The I2C interface connections are pin 1: GND, pin 2: VCC, pin 3: SDA, pin 4: SCL, and pin 5–8: No Connection. These will work with SPI and analog interfaces also.

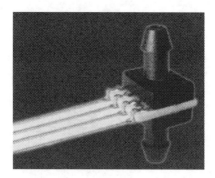

Figure 2-25. *Honeywell pressure sensor*

Air Pressure Sensor MPS20N0040D 40KPa (Differential Pressure)

The air pressure sensors shown in Figure 2-26 measure the pressure over the environment in which they are installed and transfer the information as a multivolt signal. The multivolt is collected along three output pins out of six; two more pins are input, and one is no connection. These sensors possess high reliability at low cost and use the MEMS technology. Also, they are easy to use and install in OEM equipment.

Figure 2-26. *Air pressure sensor*

Stainless Steel Pressure Transducer Sensor

This sensor consists of stainless steel with a cable of length of 19cm, as shown in Figure 2-27. The connections are three wires with red for power supply, black for ground, and yellow for output. Corrosion resistance, welded seals, high tensile strength, durability, and hardness are a few of the benefits of these type of sensors. Five types of stainless steel used in pressure transducer sensors are ferritic, austenitic, martensitic, precipitation-harden martensitic, and duplex.

Figure 2-27. *Pressure transducer sensor*
Source: https://robu.in/wp-content/uploads/2021/01/Stainless-Steel-Pressure-Transducer-Sensor-3.png

Pressure Sensor Specifications

Table 2-5 lists the specification of pressure sensors with pressure sensing ranges.

Table 2-5. *Specifications of Pressure Sensors*

Pressure Sensor	Pressure Sensing Range
BMP180 digital pressure sensor	300Pa to 1100hPa
Pressure transmitter sensor	Vacuum to 1000 bar
Honeywell HSCSAAN010ND2A3 sensor	±0.36PSI (±2.49kPa)
Air pressure sensor MPS20N0040D	0 to 5.8 psi (40kpa)
Stainless steel pressure transducer sensor	0MPa to 1.2MPa

Applications

The following are the applications of this type of sensor:

- Enhancement of GPS navigation

- Weather forecast

- Air flow monitors, flow calibrators

- Tire pressure, car air pump

- Pressure detection in oil tank and gas tank

Gas Sensors

Gas sensors can infer the presence of any gas with certain parameters in its environment. The concentration of a particular gas over the atmospheric air influences the change in any characteristics such as resistance, current, and voltage of sensor. The output directly depicts the concentration of the gas. The sensor selection is based on the concentration range of the specific gas, the nature of application, and an accuracy requirement.

MQ135: Air Quality Gas Sensor

MQ gas sensors are a type of air quality sensor that detects the presence of gases such as benzene, ammonia, alcohol, carbon dioxide, etc. The connections with the master microcontroller are through four pins: power supply, ground, digital output, and analog output (as depicted in Figure 2-28). The sensor needs to be preheated before initiating the operation to generate an accurate result. Based on the concentration of the gas, the output LED will glow.

Figure 2-28. *Air quality gas sensor*
Source: https://robu.in/wp-content/uploads/2021/07/gas-and-dust-sensor-2.jpg

AO-03 Gas Sensor

The sensor depicted in Figure 2-29 is capable of sensing the presence of oxygen. It is an electrochemical type, is portable, and is simple to deploy and replace. It produces a linear output for 0 to 30% of oxygen and nonlinear output above 30 percent. It is mainly used to detect the presence of oxygen in coal mines and in air purifiers. No external power supply is required. The two pins are Vsensor- and Vsensor+ for interfacing, as shown in Figure 2-29.

Figure 2-29. *AO-03 gas sensor*
Source: https://robu.in/wp-content/uploads/2021/11/
AO-03%E4%B8%BB%E5%9B%BE-1.jpg

TGS2610: Liquefied Petroleum Gas Sensor

The presence of liquefied petroleum gas is sensed by the TGS2610 gas sensor, which has very high sensitivity. Its low power consumption and quick response time makes it suitable for gas leakage detection. The sensor has four pins, as shown in Figure 2-30, for interfacing. Two are input voltages; one is for heater (VH), and the other is for circuit (VC). The measurement voltage and ground are the other two pins, as shown in Figure 2-30. The purpose of the integrated heater voltage is to maintain the sensing element at an optimal temperature for better sensing.

Figure 2-30. *Liquefied petroleum gas (LPG) sensor*
Source: https://robu.in/wp-content/uploads/2023/01/GAS-AND-
DUST-SENSOR-2.jpg

Toluene Electrochemical Gas Detection Module: ME3-C7H8 gas sensor

The ME3-C7H8, as shown in Figure 2-31, is an electrochemical sensor that measures the concentration of gas based on the oxidation process of detecting gas on the electrodes in the sensor. The current generated is directly proportional to the concentration of the gas. This sensor has the best repeatability and stability, high sensitivity, and precision.

Figure 2-31. *ME3-C7H8 gas sensor*
Source: https://robu.in/wp-content/uploads/2022/06/Winsen-
ME3-O3-Gas-Sensor.jpg

MQ-5B: 24V LPG Propane Methane Combustible Flammable Liquefied Gas Sensor

The MQ-5B sensor depicted in Figure 2-32 measures the concentration of flammable gases such as butane and methane at the same time. It also detects LPG (propane) with high sensitivity. The sensing material is tin oxide (SnO_2), which has less conductivity over clean air. The conductivity of the sensor increases when the concentration of flammable gas is higher in the air. The sensor measures the presence of gas with two input voltages: Vh, which is heater voltage for operating the sensor across pins 2 and 5, and Vc, which is supply voltage across pins 4 and 6. The output voltage depicts the concentration of the gas across pins 1 and 3.

Figure 2-32. *MQ-5B, 24V liquefied gas sensor*

Specifications of Gas Sensors

Table 2-6 shows the detection range of each gas sensor.

Table 2-6. *Specifications of Gas Sensors*

Gas Sensor	Detection Range
MQ135, air quality gas sensor	10 to 1000 ppm
AO-03 gas sensor	1 to 25% Vol. O_2
TGS2610, LPG sensor	1 to 25% LEL
Toluene electrochemical gas detection module, C7H8 gas sensor	0 to 100ppm
MQ-5B, 24V LPG propane methane combustible flammable liquefied gas sensor	300 to 10000ppm (CH4,C3H8)

Applications

The following are the applications of this type of sensor:

- Used in gas detection device

- Measures oxygen that exits the engine

- Residential LP leak detectors and alarms

- Used in gas detection equipment

- Detects flammable gases

Accelerometers

An accelerometer is an electromechanical that measures the forces that cause acceleration, either statically or dynamically. Gravity force is an example of static force, and any movement or shaking is an example of dynamic force. These devices are capable of measuring the acceleration over three axes. There are two working principles; one is with capacitor plates that are either fixed or attached with springs, and the capacitance changes if the plates vibrate, which in turn determines the acceleration. Another way is the sensing element is surrounded by tiny crystals of piezo electric materials, which generate electrical current if subjected to any stress or acceleration.

MPU6050: Triple Axis Gyro Accelerometer

The MPU6050 consists of an accelerometer with three axes and a gyroscope with three axes. It is based on the micro electro-mechanical system (MEMS), which measures acceleration, orientation, velocity, and other motions in any direction. The calculations are complex as it handles motion in all three axes; a digital motion processor helps with this. This sensor also has a 16-bit analog-to-digital converter (ADC), which enables the capturing of 3D motion at a time. The I2C interface is used to connect the sensor with the microcontroller with SDA and SCL pins, as shown in Figure 2-33.

Figure 2-33. *MPU6050 accelerometer*
Source: https://robu.in/wp-content/uploads/2014/12/ IMG_0379.jpg

LIS2DHTR Accelerometer

The accelerometer LIS2DHTR belongs to the Femto family, which has 14-pin interfacing, as shown in Figure 2-34. The connection between the sensor and the host processor is through either the I2C or SPI interface. The sensing acceleration range can be dynamically configured, and output data rates range from 1Hz to 5.3kHz. These devices have a self-test capability, which enables the users to verify the functionality after deployment. Also, two types of independent interrupt generation are possible: wake-up or freefall events and position.

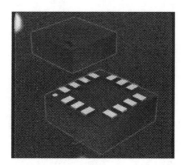

Figure 2-34. *LIS2DHTR accelerometer*

TE Connectivity 805-0500 Accelerometer

The MEAS 805-0500 sensor combines piezoceramic crystals with a charge converter amplifier enclosed in a shielded casing, which makes it well suited for OEM applications. It is available in two configurations such as adhesive type and stud type. The integrated electronic piezoelectrical (IEPE) interfacing is most common in industrial sensors. It consists of three pins. Among the three pins, pin 1 is analog output, pin 2 is ground, and pin 3 is no connection, as shown in Figure 2-35.

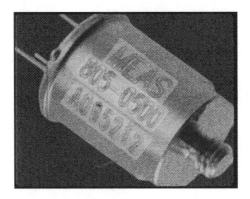

Figure 2-35. *805-0500 accelerometer*

ADXL335 Accelerometer

The ADXL335 accelerometer shown in Figure 2-36 is a common device to measure the acceleration along three dimensions. The output signal of the module is proportional to the acceleration of the object in which a sensor is mounted. It consists of capacitance plates with fixed and movable forms to determine the value of acceleration. There are five pins among which three are providing the x-axis, y-axis, and z-axis analog output; the other two pins are ground and power supply. The three outputs are used to calculate the tilt or orientation of the object. Further, angle of rolls, pitch, and yaw with respect to three axes can be calculated.

Figure 2-36. *ADXL335 accelerometer*
Source: https://robu.in/wp-content/uploads/2016/03/
61F5gkx2PGL._SX342_.jpg

BMA400: Three-Axis Digital Accelerometer

This sensor is equipped with 12-bit three-axis acceleration with interrupt triggered based on its position and motion. It can recognize any activity such as running, walking, and simply standing. The two-wire I2C interface enables the transmission of acceleration data to the master processor. Two more pins are ground and power supply, as shown in Figure 2-37. The sensor has three power modes: sleep mode, normal mode, and low-power mode. Auto wake-up functionality is also the part of the power mode, which conveys or communicates the host processor when the sensor changes from low-power mode to normal mode.

Figure 2-37. *BMA400 accelerometer*

Auto wake-up can be either time triggered or activity triggered.

Accelerometer Specifications

Table 2-7 lists the acceleration range of the accelerometers discussed earlier.

Table 2-7. *Specifications of Accelerometers*

Accelerometer	Acceleration Range
MPU6050: triple axis gyro accelerometer	±2g, ±4g, ±8g and ±16g (Gyro: ±250, ±500, ±1000, and ±2000dps)
LIS2DHTR	±2g, 4g, 8g, 16g
TE connectivity 805-0500 accelerometer	500 g
ADXL335	±3g
Seeed Studio Grove: three-axis digital accelerometer for BMA400	±16g

Applications

The following are the applications of this type of sensor:

- Wearable projects

- Freefall detection

- Machine monitoring

- Sports and health devices

- Activity tracking apps

Level Sensors

Level sensors are devices to detect the level of any substance in liquid forms mostly in any closed or open systems. There are two types of level sensors: point-level sensors and continuous-level sensors. Continuous-level sensors are able to check for the level over a range until it reaches the sensor. The point-level sensor is able to check at one point whether the substance reaches that level or not. The output will be transmitted to the monitoring host for further actions through wireless transmission also if required. Level sensors are further classified into optical, capacitance, and ultrasonic level sensors.

Water-Level Depth Detection Sensor

The water-level sensor shown in Figure 2-38 monitors the water level as an analog signal output. It can interface with the analog pin of the master controller or be fed to ADC to get digital output. It has several exposed traces arranged in parallel to each other to detect the water volume. The three pins are ground, power supply, and analog output, as shown in Figure 2-38.

Figure 2-38. *Water-level depth detection sensor*
Source: `https://robu.in/wp-content/uploads/2016/03/`
`51ENYeKOQOL.jpg`

XKC-Y25 NPN Intelligent Noncontact Liquid Water-Level Sensor

This sensor is a contactless and intelligent water-level sensor that employs signal processing technology through a high-speed processing chip. It can detect the level of various substances such as acids, alkali, and liquids stored in airtight containers. It is featured with high stability and sensitivity and also robust against electromagnets. There are four pins, namely, VCC, ground, output, and the ADJ-sensitivity adjustment switch, as shown in Figure 2-39.

Figure 2-39. *XKC-Y25 noncontact water-level sensor*
Source: `https://robu.in/wp-content/uploads/2021/05/XKC-Y25-`
`NPN-Intelligent-Non-Contact-Liquid-Water-Level-Sensor.jpeg`

Anti-Corrosion Water-Level Sensor with Ball Float Switch

The water-level sensor with a ball float switch senses the water level mounted within a tank or reservoir (see Figure 2-40). If there is no liquid in the reservoir, the sensor is in open state, and if the liquid level reaches the sensor, it is in closed state. This sensor is simple to use with no external power supply, a smaller size, and longer life.

Figure 2-40. *Anti-corrosion water-level sensor*
Source: https://robu.in/wp-content/uploads/2017/04/robu-7-1.jpg

The two-pin interfacing is with ground and digital out.

Level Sensor Specifications

Table 2-8 shows the specifications.

Table 2-8. *Specifications of Level Sensors*

Level Sensor	Detection Area
Water-level depth detection sensor	40mm × 16mm
XKC-Y25 NPN intelligent noncontact liquid water-level sensor	0mm to 20mm
Anti-corrosion water-level sensor with ball float switch	0mm to 5mm

Applications

The following are the applications of this type of sensor:

- Marine-level measurement

- Drone irrigation

- Hydroponics, saltwater tank

Summary

This chapter discussed the various types of sensors such as temperature sensors, humidity sensors, proximity sensors, infrared sensors, pressure sensors, gas sensors, accelerometers, and level sensors. The chapter also listed the specifications of the sensors so you can understand the physical parameters measured by the sensor. Also, we explained the applications of each sensor type. With this knowledge about sensors, you will be able to easily implement the communication protocols in the next chapter.

CHAPTER 3

Communication Protocols

Machines on their own can perform only limited functions. Machines that are not connected and cannot communicate with other machines are simply considered inoperable nowadays. Machines always need to be connected to communicate their status, receiving controls and other machines' status to achieve any task. The communication between machines is governed by a set of protocols depending on the communication techniques a machine supports. These protocols are a set of rules outlining the syntax and semantics of the communication and synchronizing the communicating machines with the help of software and/or hardware. This communication can be broadly classified into wired and wireless. We will discuss some standard wired communication techniques in this chapter.

Wired

Wired communication techniques can be used between two devices or between a device and its components. The devices can be personal computers, laptops, and embedded boards with MCUs. The components can be any sensors or actuators without processing capability that simply transfer data based on clock signals or triggers. The wired communication

© G.R. Kanagachidambaresan, Bharathi N. 2023
G.R. Kanagachidambaresan and N. Bharathi, *Sensors and Protocols for Industry 4.0*,
Maker Innovations Series, https://doi.org/10.1007/978-1-4842-9007-1_3

protocols Integrated Circuit (I2C), Serial Peripheral Interface (SPI), Universal Asynchronous Receiver/Transmitter (UART), and Universal Serial Bus (USB) are the ones most widely used.

I2C

The I2C protocol can connect multiple masters with one or more slaves. Also, it supports the usual single master with multiple slaves. This protocol was developed by Philips in 1980 and is pronounced "eye-squared-see" or "eye-to-see." It communicates with two wires, namely, serial data (SDA) and serial clock (SCL). The clock signal is always generated by the master device, and the slaves need to be properly synchronized with the master to receive and send signals. The data frame size is 1 byte with limited speeds over a single line for transmitting as well as receiving. Though communication is achieved with only two lines, it can support up to 1,000 devices when they don't communicate often. Since the transmission is through a single bus, adding new devices is simple, but noise sensitivity increases with the devices. The communication is half-duplex with acknowledgment at each data transmission.

Program

The `Wire.h` library needs to be installed to implement I2C communication between two devices with one as the master and one as the slave. The Tools menu in the Arduino IDE has a menu item called Manage Libraries, as shown in Figure 3-1. The Library Manager pop-up window shows all the libraries available.

Figure 3-1. *Manage Libraries menu item in the Tools menu to install the desired library*

The keyword *wire* must be typed in the search box to check whether the Wire.h library is already installed. If it is already installed, it is indicated as installed near the library, as shown in Figure 3-2. Otherwise, the library needs to be installed by clicking the Install button on the right side.

The library is called the *wire utility* library and is specific to I2C communication. Another way of installing Wire.h is to download the entire library from GitHub and store it in the Arduino library folder. The Wire.h library has several functions, as follows:

- begin(): This initializes the wire library as a peripheral or controller.

- beginTransmission(): This starts the transmission with the I2C peripheral device.

- write(): The bytes are queued for transmission through the I2C data line.

- endTransmission(): After a call to write(), this function actually transmits the data.

- read(): This function is called in the peripheral device to receive the information from the controller or read a byte of information transferred from a peripheral to a controller in response to the function call requestFrom().

- onReceive(): This function registers a user-defined function that needs to be called in the peripheral upon receiving information from the controller.

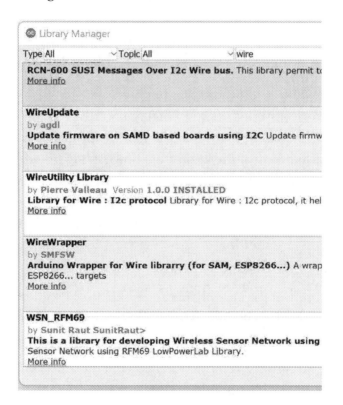

Figure 3-2. *Library Manager in the Arduino IDE*

I2C Master

Figure 3-3 shows the communication and connection establishment between the I2C master and the Arduino Uno and I2C slave and Arduino Nano.

Figure 3-3. *Arduino Uno communication with Arduino Nano using I2C*

The header file should be included in the program to call the functions defined in the Wire.h library. The following statement in the program is to enable communication using I2C in Arduino.

```
#include <Wire.h>
```

The slave address (Arduino Nano) is specified using the previous program statement, which is processed by the preprocessor and assigns address 9 to the constant S_ADDR.

```
#define S_ADDR 9
```

Analog pin 0 is assigned to read the data signal from the potentiometer using the variable Pot_Pin. After reading the data from the potentiometer, the data needs to be stored in the local variable Pot_val, which is of type integer.

```
int Pot_Pin = 0;
int Pot_val = 0;
```

The two main and necessary functions in the Arduino IDE are setup() and loop(). The setup() function initializes all the necessary communications and processing variables to accomplish the task. The I2C communication has been initialized with the previous program statements. The Arduino Uno as a master begins the transmission by calling the function begin().

```
void setup() {
    Wire.begin();
}
```

The next necessary function in the program is loop(), which continuously executes the program statements in an iterative fashion.

```
void loop() {
  delay(500);
    val = map(analogRead(Pot_Pin), 0, 1023, 255, 1);
  // Write the Potentiometer reading as character to send to
    Arduino Nano.
  Wire.beginTransmission(S_ADDR);
  Wire.write(Pot_val);
  Wire.endTransmission();
}
```

The function delay is called for a 500-millisecond delay. It is required for any task to understand the continuous flow of actions. Next, the potentiometer is accessed, and its value is read. The 10-bit value read from analog pin 0 is in the range of 0 to 1023. This needs to be mapped to the range supported by the potentiometer, i.e., 255 to 1, which can be represented using 8 bits. The built-in map() function will do the mapping. It has five parameters: the value needing to be mapped, the low value of the current range, the high value of the current range, the low value of mapping range, and the high value of mapping range. In this program, those five values are Pot_Pin, 0, 1023, 255, and 1, respectively. After reading and converting the potentiometer value, the Arduino transfers the value to the I2C slave by initiating the transmission using Wire.beginTransmission(S_ADDR). The address of the slave is passed as an argument to the function. The Wire.write(Pot_val) method writes the value, and it is ready for transmission through the I2C data line. Finally, the transmission is completed with the function call Wire.endTransmission().

I2C Slave

The header Wire.h is required to enable the I2C communication between two machines. Hence, it is added to make use of its library functions.

```
#include <Wire.h>
```

The slave I2C address is defined using the #define statement. The purpose of #define is to act as a placeholder that replaces all occurrences of SLAVE_ADDR with 9. The slave address can be a 7-bit number range from 1 to 127.

```
#define SLAVE_ADDR 9
```

The built-in pin 13 in Arduino Nano is used for LED blinking with a delay in proportion to the potentiometer value received from the I2C master. It is declared as a variable LED to write the mapped or converted potentiometer value that maps to the LED blinking rate.

```
int LED = 13;
int rd;
int br;
```

The variable rd is for receiving the I2C master data, and the variable br is for declaring the LED blink rate. Both variables are of type integer for holding the potentiometer value and the delay for blinking the LED.

The setup() function initializes all the parameters required in the loop() function.

```
void setup() {
    pinMode(LED, OUTPUT);
    Wire.begin(SLAVE_ADDR);
    Wire.onReceive(receiveEvent);
    Serial.begin(9600);
  Serial.println("I2C Slave Demonstration");
}
```

The LED mode is set to output mode using the pinMode() function. The I2C slave communication is initialized with Wire.begin(SLAVE_ADDR). A function receiveEvent() is initialized for execution when the data is received from the I2C master with Wire.onReceive() by passing an argument.

The Serial Monitor is initialized with the baud rate of 9600 bits per second as Serial.begin() for displaying the potentiometer values for the users. The first statement "I2C Slave Demonstration" in the Serial Monitor is printed with Serial.println(), as shown in Figure 3-4.

Figure 3-4. *Communication demonstration at slave*

The function receiveEvent() is defined to read the data from the I2C data line and print it in the Serial Monitor.

```
void receiveEvent() {
        rd = Wire.read();
        Serial.println(rd);
        delay(500);
}
```

The function reads a character from I2C using the function Wire.read(). The Serial.println() function is called to display the received value from the I2C data line. Finally, the delay function is called to perform no operation for the next 500 milliseconds.

Generally, the function loop() is defined to repeat the actions continuously. In this application, the function map() is called to convert the value in the range 1 to 255 to the range 100 to 2000. It is to proportionately calculate the blink rate or delay value in milliseconds based on the received potentiometer value. With the computed blink rate, the LED is turned ON and OFF by sending HIGH and LOW signals through the output line with a delay of a computed blinking rate between two states.

```
void loop() {
  br = map(rd, 1, 255, 100, 2000);
  digitalWrite(LED, HIGH);
 delay(br);
 digitalWrite(LED, LOW);
 delay(br);
 }
```

Connection Details

Table 3-1 shows the connection details between the Arduino Uno, Arduino Nano, and 10K Preset.

Table 3-1. *Connection Details for I2C*

Arduino Uno (Master)	Arduino Nano (Slave)	10k Preset (Potentiometer)
Pin A4 (SDA)	Pin A4 (SDA)	-
Pin A5 (SCL)	Pin A5 (SCL)	-
GND	GND	-
Pin A0	-	Vout
5V	-	5V
GND	-	GND
-	LED_BUILTIN (pin 13 in Nano)	-

I2C Interfacing with Raspberry Pi

The 16-bit analog-to-digital converter ADS1115 interfaces with the Raspberry Pi through I2C.

The ADS1115 shown in Figure 3-5 supports four channels through which analog sensors can be connected with single-board computers such as the Raspberry Pi, as shown in Figure 3-6. The machines are monitored and controlled with analog and digital sensors. The values of sensors can be read and viewed in a graph or in Google Sheets. This section demonstrates the interfacing of ADS1115 with the Raspberry Pi.

Figure 3-5. *ADS1115*

Figure 3-6. *Raspberry Pi*

The connection details of the Raspberry Pi with ADS1115 are as follows:

ADS1115 VDD: Raspberry Pi 3.3V

ADS1115 GND: Raspberry Pi GND

ADS1115 SCL: Raspberry Pi SCL

ADS1115 SDA: Raspberry Pi SDA

The required libraries for connecting to a Google spreadsheet for remote monitoring, displaying date and time, generating a delay (time), displaying a graph locally, and utilizing ADS1115 functionalities are imported into the code.

```
import gspread
import datetime
import time
import matplotlib.pyplot as plt
import Adafruit_ADS1x15
```

The Google spreadsheet is accessed through Python code with the appropriate credentials. The sheet is opened and assigned to the handle, which can be used to update the cells in the sheet.

```
from google.oauth2.service_account import Credentials
scope = ['https://www.googleapis.com/auth/spreadsheets',
        'https://www.googleapis.com/auth/drive']
creds = Credentials.from_service_account_file("credentials.
json", scopes=scope)
gc = gspread.authorize(creds)
wks = gc.open("ADS_to_Gspread").sheet1
```

The values that are read through ADS1115 are plotted locally by creating a plot with interactive mode turned on. The four subplots are created within the global plot for four channels of ADS1115. The x value is common to all the subplots, and the y value is the data read through four channels using y, y1, y2, and y3, respectively.

```
plt.ion()
x=[]
y=[]
y1=[]
y2=[]
y3=[]
fig,((ax1,ax2),(ax3,ax4)) = plt.subplots(2,2,num='ADS1115
Demonstration')
fig.suptitle('ADS output from 4 Analog sensors',fontsize=12)
```

The graph is generated with common x values for all subplots and separate y values for each subplot. The subplots are differentiated with a separate title and color assigned.

```
def graph(temp, temp1, temp2, temp3):
    y.append(temp)
    y1.append(temp1)
    y2.append(temp2)
    y3.append(temp3)
    x.append(time.time())
    ax1.plot(x,y)
    ax1.set_title("Sensor1", fontsize=8);
    ax2.plot(x,y1,'tab:orange')
    ax2.set_title("Sensor2", fontsize=8);
    ax3.plot(x,y2,'tab:green')
    ax3.set_title("Sensor3", fontsize=8);
    ax4.plot(x,y3,'tab:red')
```

85

```
ax4.set_title("Sensor4", fontsize=8);
for ax in fig.get_axes():
    ax.label_outer()
```

The ADC instance adc is created, and the gain value is assigned as 1 for reading voltages from 0 to 4.09V. The four columns are formatted using a print statement to display the four channel values in the command prompt. The column headers are displayed as 0, 1, 2, and 3, respectively.

```
# Create an ADS1115 ADC (16-bit) instance.
adc = Adafruit_ADS1x15.ADS1115()
GAIN = 1
print('Reading ADS1115 values, press Ctrl-C to quit'…')
# Print nice channel column headers.
pri't('| {0:>6} | {1:>6} | {2:>6} | {3:>6'
|'.format(*range(4)))
pri't''-' * 37)
```

The values are read through the adc instance by calling the read_adc() method. All the ADC channel values are read in a list. A delay of two seconds is generated by calling sleep(2) for demonstration purposes.

```
j=1
while True:
    values = [0]*4
    for I in range(0,4):
        values[i] = adc.read_adc(i, gain=GAIN)
    print''| {0:>6} | {1:>6} | {2:>6} | {3:>6}
    ''.format(*values))
    # Pause for 2 seconds.
    time.sleep(2)
```

The Google spreadsheet is updated with the date and time in the first column followed by the four values in the successive columns of the same row. Figure 3-7 shows that the command prompt contains the values displayed in a formatted manner. Figure 3-8 shows the graph plotted locally in order to monitor the behavior of the analog sensors connected. Figure 3-9 shows the Google spreadsheet updated and its corresponding graph dynamically updating its content.

```
temp = str(datetime.datetime.now())
    wks.update_cell(j, 1, temp)
    for k in range(0,4):
        wks.update_cell(j, k+2, str(values[k]))
    graph(values[0],values[1],values[2],values[3])
    j=j+1
    plt.pause(1)
```

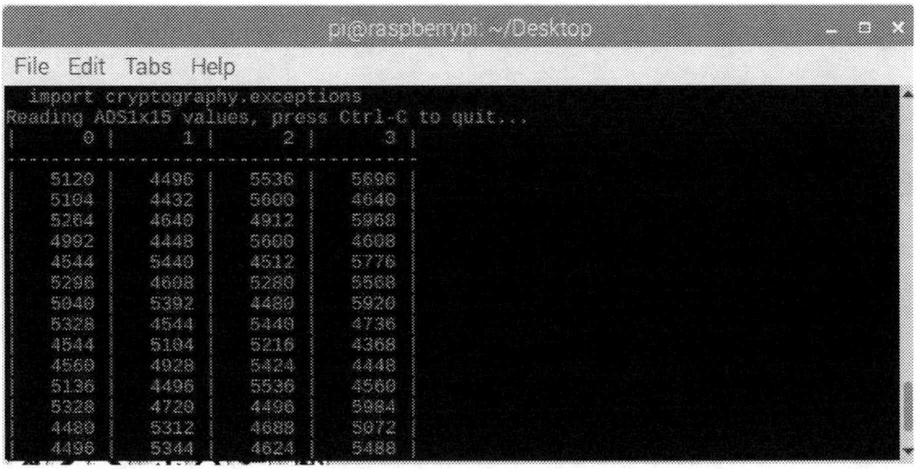

Figure 3-7. *Four channel values from ADS1115*

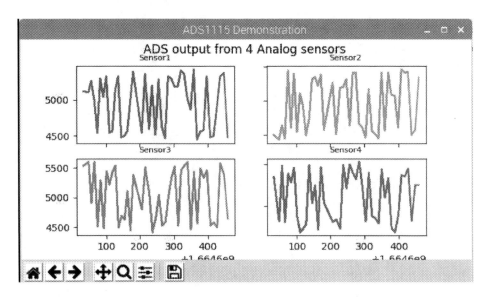

Figure 3-8. *Four-channel output plotted in four subplots*

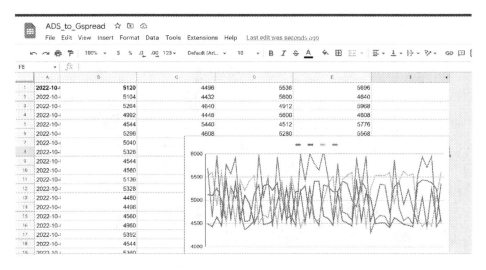

Figure 3-9. *Remote monitoring of four-channel values of ADS1115 using a Google spreadsheet*

Serial Peripheral Interface

The SPI protocol was developed in the 1980s by Motorola, and it supports a single master with multiple slaves. It uses four wires to communicate using full-duplex mode. Slave Select (SS) is used to identify the slave device, Master Out Slave In (MOSI) is for transmission from slave to master, Master In Slave Out (MISO) is for transmission from master to slave, and Serial Clock (SCLK) is used for synchronization, which is always controlled by the master. The constraint in this protocol is that each slave SS line is required separately from the master to the newly added slave. Hence, a multiplexer can be used to resolve this constraint. The data rate is generally high since it supports full-duplex mode with no start and stop bits. The communication is smooth with less noise sensitivity and no acknowledgment at each transmission.

Program

The SPI devices require the header file `SPI.h`, which is one of the core libraries in Arduino, and hence a separate installation is not needed. This library has the following functions to establish communication and transfer data:

- `begin()`: This function initializes the interface by configuring the SCK, MOSI, and SS to outputs.

- `setClockDivider(divider)`: This function sets the SPI clock divider with respect to the system clock. The divider constants are `SPI_CLOCK_DIV2`, `SPI_CLOCK_DIV4`, `SPI_CLOCK_DIV8`, `SPI_CLOCK_DIV16`, `SPI_CLOCK_DIV32`, `SPI_CLOCK_DIV64`, and `SPI_CLOCK_DIV128`, which divide the system clock by 2, 4, 8, 16, 32, 64, and 128, respectively.

- `transfer(val)`: The SPI data transfer is implemented on simultaneous send and receive. The received data is stored in a buffer or returned to the `receivedVal`.

- `beginTransaction()`: This initializes the SPI bus using the SPI settings. The SPI setting is an object whose values configure the SPI port. It has three variables. `speedMaximum` is the speed of communication up to a maximum of 20MHz. `dataOrder` is the order of data specified with either the most significant byte first or the least significant byte first. `dataMode` consists of four modes; namely, `SPI_MODE0`, `SPI_MODE1`, `SPI_MODE2`, and `SPI_MODE3` are used for controlling the data out or in during the falling or rising edge of the clock.

- `attachInterrupt()`: This function attaches the interrupt service routine (ISR) with SPI communication. The attached ISR is called and executed when the interrupt occurred. ISR is special type of function that receives no parameter and returns nothing. Instead, the control and data registers are modified based on the status of SPI communication. The variables used inside the ISR should be global and volatile to communicate with the main program.

SPI Master

Figure 3-10 shows the communication and connection establishment between the SPI master and Arduino Uno and the I2C slave and Arduino Nano.

Figure 3-10. *Arduino Uno communication with Arduino Nano using SPI*

The header SPI.h is required to enable serial peripheral communication between two machines. Hence, it is added to make use of its library functions.

```
#include <SPI.h>
```

The setup() function is defined to initialize the parameters used in the loop() function. The baud rate is initialized to 115200 bits/s for the UART communication. The SS pin is initialized to a low signal because a slave select signal needs to be disabled initially in the master. The begin() function is called to configure the serial peripheral interface communication pins and establish communication. The function setClockDivider() sets the SPI clock divider with respect to the system (e.g., Arduino UNO) clock.

```
void setup (void) {
    Serial.begin(115200);
    digitalWrite(SS, HIGH);
    SPI.begin ();
    SPI.setClockDivider(SPI_CLOCK_DIV8);
}
```

The loop() function will repeat the execution for continuously transferring the message to the slave from the master. The slave select signal needs to be enabled before communication by sending a low value to the SS pin. Now the message needs to be sent to the slave using the transfer() function in the SPI library. The characters are transferred one by one as the communication is serial. The characters are converted to binary codes and transmitted bit by bit, internally. After transmitting the message, the slave select signal needs to be disabled. The delay function is called to separate the two successive messages for five seconds. Hence, communication using an SPI interface is implemented from the master device.

```
void loop (void) {
   char c;
   digitalWrite(SS, LOW);
   for (const char * tstr = "SPI communication demonstration\r"
   ; c = *tstr; tstr++)
   {
      SPI.transfer (c);
      Serial.print(c);
   }
   digitalWrite(SS, HIGH);
   delay(5000);
}
```

SPI Slave

The serial communication is established with the set of functions that are defined in the library called SPI.h, and hence it needs to be included into the code.

```
#include <SPI.h>
```

The buffer to receive the message needs to be declared with the size of the buffer.

```
char buff [60];
volatile byte mess_idx;
volatile boolean flag_process;
```

Generally, the buffer is of the character data type, and the size in this demonstration is declared as 60. Each character in the receiving message is added into the buffer successively by incrementing the index of the character buffer (array). The volatile qualifier is specified during the declaration of the variable before the datatype. It is a compiler directive to instruct the compiler to retrieve the variable value from RAM instead of a storage register. There are two reasons to declare it as volatile. First, when the variable is stored in register, the value may be inaccurate under abnormal conditions though this rarely occurs. Second, if the variable is declared as volatile, then it can be changed outside of the actual code section where it belongs. It is required when interrupts are handled with interrupt service routines (ISRs) and also during execution of concurrent threads in certain applications. In this code section, the variables mess_idx and flag_process are declared as byte and Boolean datatypes along with the qualifier volatile in order to access the ISR.

```
void setup (void) {
    Serial.begin (115200);
    pinMode(MISO, OUTPUT);
    SPCR |= _BV(SPE);
    mess_idx = 0;
    flag_process = false;
    SPI.attachInterrupt();
}
```

The setup() function is used to initialize the parameters required to establish the communication and enable them to receive messages from the master. The begin() function configures the baud rate for communication as 115200 bits/s. The pinMode() function sets the MISO pin of the slave as an output pin to send information to the master through this pin. The SPCR is the SPI control register, which is 8-bit (0 to 7). Bits 7 and 6 are SPI interrupt enable and SPI enable. To enable SPI, SPCR |= _BV(SPE) is used. _BV(SPE) is defined as follows:

```
#define _BV(bit) (1 << (bit))
```

Hence, in this code segment, it is (1<<(SPE)), i.e., six times left shift of binary 1 to make 01000000B on the right side of the equation. Then it is bitwise ORed with SPCR, and hence SPI is enabled.

The volatile variables mess_idx and flag_process are initialized to 0 and false as the communication is yet to start. Finally, the SPI interrupt is attached with the ISR by calling the function attachInterrupt().

ISR is the interrupt service routine that attaches the handler of SPI to SPI_STC_vect, which is Serial Transfer Complete interrupt vector. The byte information is read from the SPI data register SPDR and stored to the byte variable data_master. The single byte data received each time is appended in the buffer of size 60 bytes by incrementing the byte array index. The received byte is checked for a carriage return, and if it is a carriage return, the processing flag is set to true to further manipulate the data in the slave.

The loop() function is for repeatedly executing the code, and hence the further processing of the master message is implemented. This function should be executed when the message is received from the master, and this is checked through the flag_process being set to true or not. If it is true, the flag needs to be reset. The message received from the master that is collected in the buffer and its content are displayed through the Serial Monitor, as shown in Figure 3-11.

Figure 3-11. *SPI demonstration of the slave*

Further, the buffer index variable mess_idx is reset to zero to receive the next message.

```
ISR (SPI_STC_vect) // Interrupt Service Routine

{

   byte data_master = SPDR;
   if (mess_idx < sizeof buff) {
      buff [mess_idx ++] = data_master; // save data in the
                                        next index in the
                                        array buff
      if (data_master == '\r') //check for the end of the word
      flag_process = true;
   }
}
void loop (void)    // Repeated forever
{
   if (flag_process) {
      flag_process = false;
      Serial.println("Slave:");
      Serial.println (buff);
```

```
      mess_idx = 0;
   }
}
```

Connection Details

Table 3-2 depicts the connection details between the Arduino Uno and Arduino Nano.

Table 3-2. *Connection Details Between Arduino Uno and Nano*

Arduino Uno (Master)	Arduino Nano (Slave)
Pin 10 (SS)	Pin D10 (SS)
Pin 11 (MOSI)	Pin D11 (MOSI)
Pin 12 (MISO)	Pin D12 (MISO)
Pin 13 (SCK)	Pin D13 (SCK)
GND	GND

SPI Interfacing with Raspberry Pi Using MCP3008

The MCP3008 supports the industry-standard SPI, which builds on a successive approximation register (SAR) architecture. It is available in 16-pin SOIC and PDIP packages, as shown in Figure 3-12. It enables 10-bit ADC, which can be interfaced with any PIC microcontroller. The MCP3008 has eight input channels, which operate at 200k samples/second and consume low power. Applications for the MCP3008 include industrial automation, data acquisition, multichannel data loggers, etc.

Figure 3-12. *MCP3008*

The connection details of the Raspberry Pi with MCP3008 are as follows:

MCP3008 VDD: Raspberry Pi 3.3V

MCP3008 VREF: Raspberry Pi 3.3V

MCP3008 AGND: Raspberry Pi GND

MCP3008 DGND: Raspberry Pi GND

MCP3008 CLK: Raspberry Pi SCLK

MCP3008 DOUT: Raspberry Pi MISO

MCP3008 DIN: Raspberry Pi MOSI

MCP3008 CS/SHDN: Raspberry Pi CE0

The required libraries for SPI and MCP3008 are gspread for updating in a Google spreadsheet and matplotlib for plotting the graph locally.

```
import gspread
import datetime
import time
import matplotlib.pyplot as plt
import Adafruit_GPIO.SPI as SPI
import Adafruit_MCP3008
```

Access to the spreadsheet to update the MCP3008's eight channels is done by calling the gspread.authorize() and gc.open() methods, respectively.

```
from google.oauth2.service_account import Credentials
scope = ['https://www.googleapis.com/auth/spreadsheets',
         'https://www.googleapis.com/auth/drive']
creds = Credentials.from_service_account_file("credentials.
json", scopes=scope)
gc = gspread.authorize(creds)
wks = gc.open("MCP_to_Gspread").sheet1}
}
```

The hardware connection establishment is set to initiate the SPI communication.

```
SPI_PORT   = 0
SPI_DEVICE = 0
mcp = Adafruit_MCP3008.MCP3008(spi=SPI.SpiDev(SPI_PORT, SPI_
DEVICE)) }
```

The graph is created as a plot, and its interactive mode is turned on in order to dynamically change its graph as and when the values are read from the MCP3008. This graph is to view locally the progress of eight channels (sensors) of MCP3008. Hence, the main plot is divided into eight subplots.

```
plt.ion()
x=[]
y=[]
y1=[]
y2=[]
y3=[]
y4=[]
```

```
y5=[]
y6=[]
y7=[]
fig,((ax1,ax2,ax3,ax4),(ax5,ax6,ax7,ax8))=plt.
subplots(2,4,num='MCP3008 Demonstration')
fig.suptitle('MCP output from 8 Analog sensors',fontsize=12)
```

Each subplot is defined by specifying its title, color of graph, x and y values, etc. There are eight subplots that display the dynamic change of each sensor value connected with each channel of MCP3008, as shown in Figure 3-14.

```
def graph(temp, temp1, temp2, temp3,temp4,temp5,temp6,temp7):
    y.append(temp)
    y1.append(temp1)
    y2.append(temp2)
    y3.append(temp3)
    y4.append(temp4)
    y5.append(temp5)
    y6.append(temp6)
    y7.append(temp7)
    x.append(time.time())
    ax1.plot(x,y)
    ax1.set_title("Sensor1", fontsize=8);
    ax2.plot(x,y1,'tab:orange')
    ax2.set_title("Sensor2", fontsize=8);
    ax3.plot(x,y2,'tab:green')
    ax3.set_title("Sensor3", fontsize=8);
    ax4.plot(x,y3,'tab:red')
    ax4.set_title("Sensor4", fontsize=8);
    ax5.plot(x,y4)
    ax5.set_title("Sensor5", fontsize=8);
```

```
ax6.plot(x,y5,'tab:blue')
ax6.set_title("Sensor6", fontsize=8);
ax7.plot(x,y6,'tab:red')
ax7.set_title("Sensor7", fontsize=8);
ax8.plot(x,y7,'tab:brown')
ax8.set_title("Sensor8", fontsize=8);
for ax in fig.get_axes():
    ax.label_outer()
```

The eight channel values are read using the method mcp.read_adc(). It is displayed in the monitor, as shown in Figure 3-13. A delay of a half-second is generated, and again the eight channels are sampled for the next set of values.

```
print('Reading MCP3008 values, press Ctrl-C to quit...')
# Print nice channel column headers.
print('| {0:>4} | {1:>4} | {2:>4} | {3:>4} | {4:>4} | {5:>4} |
{6:>4} | {7:>4} |'.format(*range(8)))
print('-' * 57)
# Main program loop.
j=1
while True:
    values = [0]*8
    for i in range(8):
        values[i] = mcp.read_adc(i)
    print('| {0:>4} | {1:>4} | {2:>4} | {3:>4} | {4:>4} |
    {5:>4} | {6:>4} | {7:>4} |'.format(*values))
    time.sleep(0.5)
```

The Google spreadsheet is updated immediately after the values are read from the MCP3008 channels. The remote monitoring of sensors is enabled by this update in the spreadsheet, as shown in Figure 3-15.

```
temp = str(datetime.datetime.now())
    wks.update_cell(j, 1, temp)
    for k in range(0,8):
        wks.update_cell(j, k+2, str(values[k]))
    graph(values[0],values[1],values[2],values[3],values[4],val
    ues[5],values[6],values[7])
    j=j+1
    plt.pause(1)
```

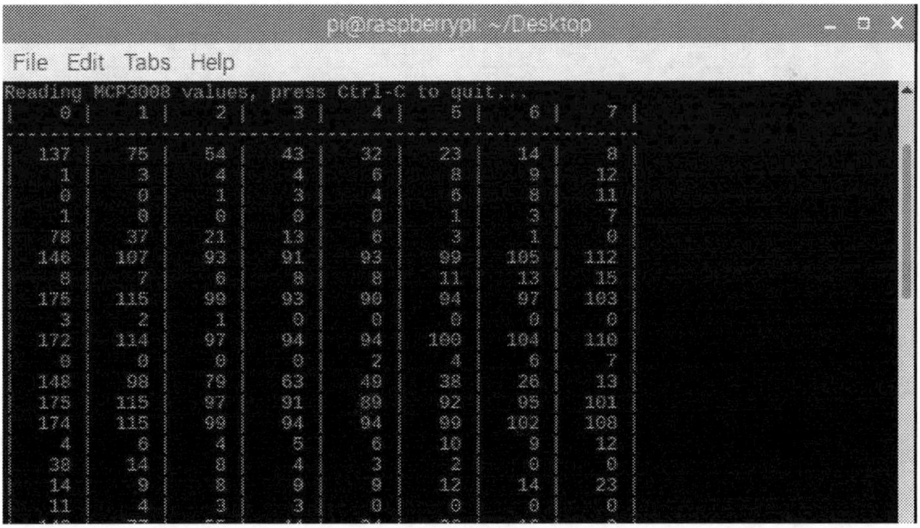

Figure 3-13. *Eight channel values from MCP3008*

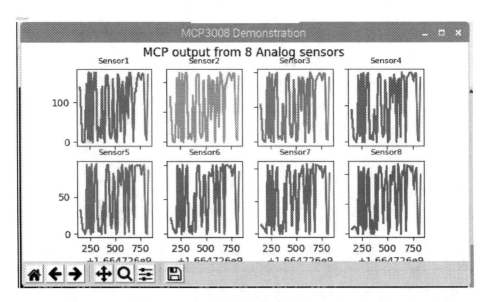

Figure 3-14. *Eight channel output plotted in eight subplots*

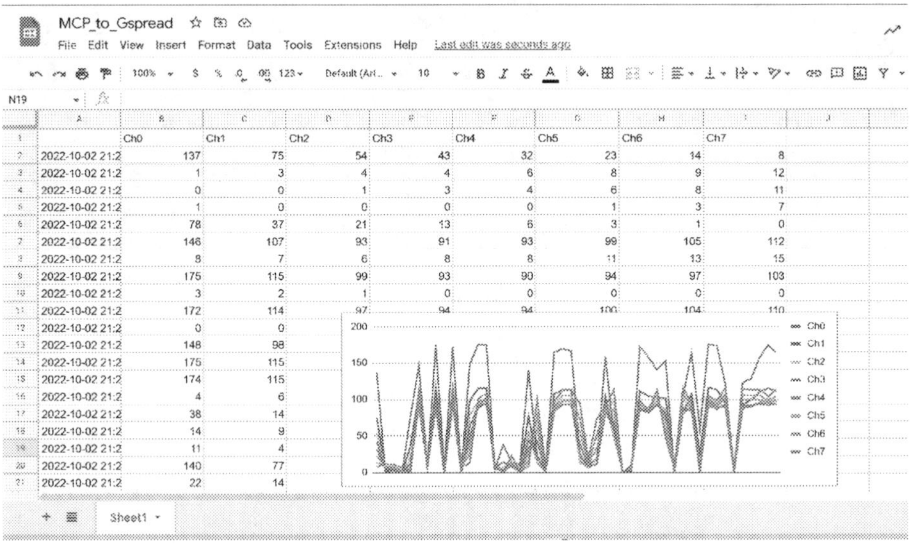

Figure 3-15. *Remote monitoring of eight channel values of MCP3008 using a Google spreadsheet*

UART

This protocol is used mainly to convert and transmit parallel data into serial. It requires only two wires: Tx pin and Rx pin. The Tx pin of the sender is connected with the Rx pin of receiver, and vice versa. No clock pulse is required as it is asynchronous communication that uses start and stop bits with the specified baud rate expressed in bits per second. The baud rate or operating frequency should be the same for both the sender and receiver. This is a one-to-one protocol that does not support multiple masters or slaves. This is inexpensive communication with a set of possible baud rates such as 9600, 19200, 38400, 57600, 115200, etc.

Here are the connection details:

> *TX pin of Arduino Nano*: RX pin of Arduino Uno
>
> *RX pin of Arduino Nano*: TX pin of Arduino Uno
>
> *GND of Arduino Nano*: GND of Arduino Uno

UART Master

The Arduino Nano is configured as a master in this demonstration, and the Arduino Uno is the slave.

The message from the master that is transmitted to the slave through UART will be displayed in the slave after receiving the message.

```
char message[20] = "Arduino Nano Master";
```

The serial communication is initiated at the master by setting the baud rate as 9600 bits per second.

```
void setup() {
 Serial.begin(9600);
}
```

The message is transmitted to the serial interface, and a delay of 1 second is generated. This is repeated as the statements are enclosed in the loop() method.

```
void loop() {
    Serial.write(message,20);
    delay(1000);
  }
```

UART Slave

The message variable is declared in the slave to receive the message, and the setup() method is defined to initialize the serial communication baud rate of 9600 bits per second.

```
char message[20];
void setup() {
    Serial.begin(9600);
  }
```

The readBytes() method is called to receive the message from the master through the UART interface, i.e., the TX and RX pins. The received message is then displayed in Serial Monitor for demonstration purposes, as shown in Figure 3-16. Alternatively, the message or data received from the master can be used to trigger any event or actuator based on the application requirements.

```
void loop() {
    Serial.readBytes(message,20);
    Serial.println("Master Message is:");
    Serial.println(message);
    delay(1000);
  }
```

Figure 3-16. *UART demonstration of the slave*

RS 485

RS485 is a serial communication interface that is similar in functionality to RS232. RS485 is faster than RS232 and supports distances of up to 1200 meters. RS485 supports the connectivity of more than one device and up to 32 devices at a time. It is less susceptible to noise as the shielding of the cable blocks the external noise. RS485 is widely used in industry for connecting machines for control and monitoring. In this demonstration, shown in Figure 3-17, the Raspberry Pi is configured as the master, and the Arduino Uno is configured as a slave. The Google spreadsheet contains the data that is sent to the Raspberry Pi from the remote location. The Raspberry Pi in turn sends the data to the local slave Arduino Uno. The Arduino Uno controls the servo motor attached to it with the data received from the Raspberry Pi i.

The connection details are as follows (RS485 is MAX485 TTL to RS485 Converter Module):

Between RS485 and Raspberry Pi

DI of RS485: GPIO14 (TX) of Raspberry Pi

DE, RE of RS485: GPIO4 of Raspberry Pi

105

RO of RS485: GPIO15(RX) of Raspberry Pi

VCC of RS485: 5V of Raspberry Pi

GND of RS485: GND of Raspberry Pi

A of RS485: To A of slave RS-485

B of RS485: To B of slave RS-485

Between RS485 and Arduino Uno

DI of RS485: 1 pin (TX) of Arduino Uno

DE, RE of RS485: 2 pin of Arduino Uno

RO of RS485: 0 pin (RX) of Arduino Uno

VCC of RS485: 5V of Arduino Uno

GND of RS485: GND of Arduino Uno

A of RS485: To A of master RS-485

B of RS485: To B of master RS-485

Between LCD and Arduino Uno

VSS of LCD: GND of Arduino Uno

VDD of LCD: +5V of Arduino Uno

V0 of LCD: To potentiometer output pin (contrast control of LCD)

RS of LCD: 8 pin of Arduino Uno

RW of LCD: GND of Arduino Uno

E of LCD: 9 pin of Arduino Uno

D4 of LCD: 10 pin of Arduino Uno

D5 of LCD: 11 pin of Arduino Uno

D6 of LCD: 12 pin of Arduino Uno

D7 of LCD: 13 pin of Arduino Uno

A of LCD: +5V of Arduino Uno

K of LCD: GND of Arduino Uno

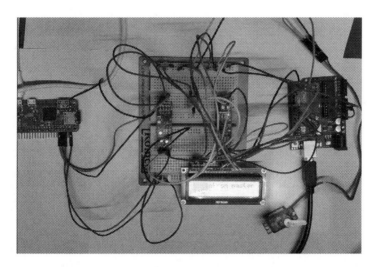

Figure 3-17. *The setup of the master Raspberry Pi 0 and slave Arduino Uno connected using RS485*

RS485 Master

The master is implemented as a Python program on the Raspberry Pi. The required modules are imported into the program. `serial` is for communication, `gspread` is for reading values from the spreadsheet, `GPIO` is for connecting the GPIO pins in the Raspberry Pi and set as output, and the `time` module is for calling the sleep function to generate a delay.

```
import time
import serial
import gspread
```

```
import RPi.GPIO as GPIO
from time import sleep

GPIO.setwarnings(False)
GPIO.setmode(GPIO.BOARD)
GPIO.setup(7, GPIO.OUT, initial=GPIO.HIGH)
```

The Google spreadsheet shown in Figure 3-18 is accessed to read the value and control the servo motor connected with the Arduino Uno slave.

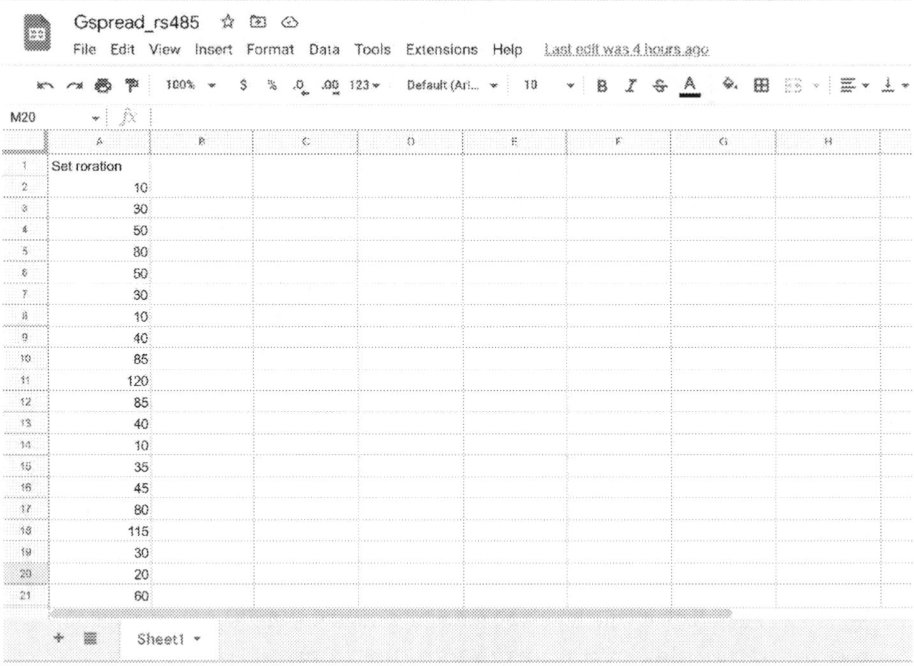

Figure 3-18. *Angle controlling values for servo motor in the Google spreadsheet*

The credentials need to be created and shared with the authorize() method, and the corresponding spreadsheet is opened using the open() method.

```
from google.oauth2.service_account import Credentials
scope = ['https://www.googleapis.com/auth/spreadsheets',
         'https://www.googleapis.com/auth/drive']
creds = Credentials.from_service_account_file("credentials.
json", scopes=scope)
gc = gspread.authorize(creds)
wks = gc.open("Gspread_rs485").sheet1
```

The serial communication handle is configured by calling the method Serial(), and the necessary parameters are passed to it.

```
send = serial.Serial( port='/dev/serial0', baudrate = 9600,
parity=serial.PARITY_NONE,
        stopbits=serial.STOPBITS_ONE,      bytesize=serial.
        EIGHTBITS,      timeout=1 )
```

The value from the spreadsheet is accessed by calling cell().value. Then the value is transmitted using the serial handler. Then a delay of 1.5 seconds is generated to synchronize with the slave. The controlling data from the spreadsheet is accessed and sent to the slave, and the process is repeated 20 times. Alternatively, it can be done forever by configuring the loop to execute infinitely.

```
r=2
c=1
while r<=20:
    x = wks.cell(r, c).value
    send.write(str.encode(str(x)))
    print(x)
    time.sleep(1.5)
    r=r+1
```

RS485 Slave

The required libraries are included in the Arduino sketch. Servo.h controls the servo motor, and LiquidCrystal.h displays the angle of control in the liquid crystal display.

```
#include <LiquidCrystal.h>
#include <Servo.h>
int enablePin = 2;
LiquidCrystal lcd(8,9,10,11,12,13);        // Define LCD display
                                           pins RS,E,D4,D5,D6,D7
Servo servo;
```

The setup() method contains the initialization of liquid crystal display, servo motor, and serial communication. The LCD is set to the initial message "Gspread control RS_485" by appropriately setting the cursor position." Serial communication is initialized by setting the baud rate as 9600 bits per second via calling the Serial.begin() method. The servo motor is attached to pin 3 of the Arduino Uno.

The loop() function contains the instructions to clear the LCD, receive the serial data from the master, and send it to the servo motor to control the angle of rotation. Finally, the angle value just rotated in the servo motor is displayed in the LCD, as shown in Figure 3-19, by setting its cursor appropriately. The process is repeated forever till the serial interface is transmitting the control data.

```
void setup()
{
  lcd.begin(16,2);
  lcd.print("Gspread control");
  lcd.setCursor(0,1);
  lcd.print("RS_485");
  delay(3000);
```

```
  lcd.clear();
  Serial.begin(9600);
  pinMode(enablePin, OUTPUT);
  delay(10);
  digitalWrite(enablePin, LOW);
  servo.attach(3);
}

void loop()
{
  while (Serial.available())                          //While have
                                                      data at Serial
                                                      port this loop
                                                      executes

    {
      lcd.clear();
      int angle = Serial.parseInt();   //Receive INTEGER
                                       value from Master
                                       throught RS-485
      servo.write(angle);                   //Write received
                                            value to
                                            Servo PWM pin
                                            (Setting Angle)

      lcd.setCursor(0,0);
      lcd.print("AngleFrom master");
      lcd.setCursor(0,1);
      lcd.print(angle);                         //Displays the
                                                Angle value

    }
  }
```

Figure 3-19. *LCD displaying the angle data received from the master*

Summary

This chapter discussed the various wired communication techniques that are used with the Internet of Things. Next, the various boards and their preferences for the application will be discussed to develop industrial IoT applications.

CHAPTER 4

Single-Board Computers

This chapter explores the benefits of the Internet of Things (IoT) for various business processes, types of communication models, and levels of IoT. It also provides insights into how to choose the best single-board computers with a quick reference of available alternatives of various components in single-board computers. Finally, various single-board computers available for IoT applications, and their features are listed.

IoT at a Glance

The IoT is a network that connects various types of devices, including computers, mechanical and digital machines, objects, animals, and even humans, each of which is assigned a unique identifier (UID) and has the capacity to exchange data with other nodes in the network independently of human intervention. Any device that can be assigned an IP address and can transfer data over a network is considered to be part of the IoT, including individuals with implanted heart monitors, animals in farms with biochip transponders, sensors in cars to alert drivers when tire air pressure is low, etc. The IoT is being used by businesses of various sizes and in a wide range of domains to streamline operations, gain insight into their customers to provide better service, boost productivity and profitability, and increase the company's overall worth.

© G.R. Kanagachidambaresan, Bharathi N. 2023
G.R. Kanagachidambaresan and N. Bharathi, *Sensors and Protocols for Industry 4.0*,
Maker Innovations Series, https://doi.org/10.1007/978-1-4842-9007-1_4

In many ways, businesses stand to gain from the advent of the IoT. There are some advantages that are applicable to only one sector, while others can be used in several. The Internet of Things allows companies to do many things, as shown in Figure 4-1.

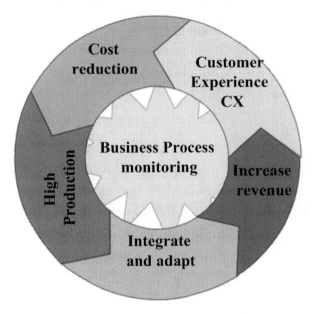

Figure 4-1. *Business process monitoring using IoT*

The IoT motivates organizations to reexamine their processes and supply them with the resources they need to enhance their operative strategy.

Sensors and other IoT devices are most common in the industrial, transportation, and utility sectors, but the IoT also has applications in the infrastructure, agriculture, and home automation domains, pushing some businesses toward digital transformation.

There are many ways in which the IoT may make life easier for farmers. Temperature, humidity, soil composition, and rainfall are just some of the variables that can be monitored by sensors to inform automated farming practices.

The Internet of Things can also aid in the monitoring of infrastructure operations. Buildings, bridges, and other infrastructure could be monitored for events or changes using sensors. There are upsides to this, including financial savings, time savings, improved workflow quality, and a reduction in paper use.

The Internet of Things can be used by a home automation company to keep tabs on the property's electrical and mechanical workings. Smart cities have the potential to greatly assist residents in cutting down on garbage and utility bills.

Everything from the medical field to the financial sector to the retail sector and even the manufacturing sector is affected by the Internet of Things.

From consumer IoT and commercial IoT to industrial and manufacturing IoT, the IoT has many practical uses. Many industries can benefit from the Internet of Things, not just the ones listed here.

In the residential market, smart houses that feature remote-controllable thermostats, smart appliances, and connected heating, lighting, and electrical devices are becoming increasingly common.

With the help of sensors and computer software, wearable devices can learn about their users and their habits and then relay that information to other devices for the purpose of streamlining and improving those users' daily lives. There are a number of ways in which wearable technology is being used to make the public safer, such as by helping emergency personnel get to a disaster site more quickly by providing them with the most direct route and by keeping tabs on the health and well-being of construction workers and firefighters while they are on the job.

One of the numerous ways in which the Internet of Things can improve healthcare is by allowing for more in-depth monitoring of patients through the examination of collected data. Inventory management of drugs and medical equipment is only another example of how IoT technologies are used in hospitals.

By employing sensors to determine the number of people present in a given space, smart buildings can cut down on unnecessary energy consumption. Sensors of a particular meeting room can activate the air conditioning when the room is full, and if the office is vacant, the regulator can be set lower.

IoT-based smart farming systems can monitor the temperature, light, humidity, and soil moisture of crop fields. The Internet of Things is also helpful in automatic irrigation systems.

Smart streetlights and smart meters are two more examples of the Internet of Things. Sensors and deployments can ease traffic, save energy, monitor and control environmental concerns, and boost cleanliness in a city.

Types of Communication on the IoT

There are a number of different types of communication models used in IoT applications: request-response model, publish-subscribe model, push-pull model, and exclusive pair model. In this section, we will briefly explain them.

Request-Response Model

The IoT device that submits a request to the server is the client. The request could be to transfer or upload data. The server may be remote or local and is capable of processing requests from numerous clients. The request-response mechanism is stateless; therefore, each request is handled independently. The server is able to receive the request, determine its answer, and retrieve the data, as shown in Figure 4-2.

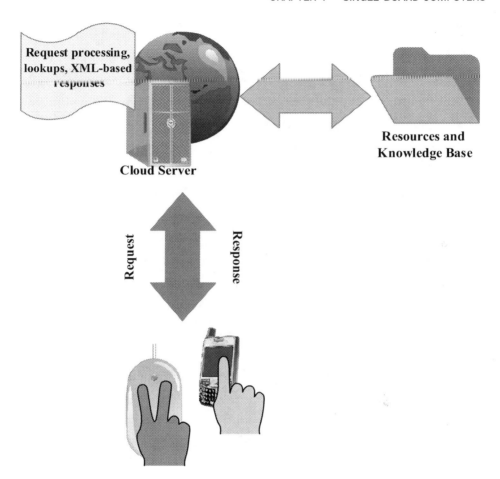

Figure 4-2. *Request-response model*

Publish-Subscribe Model

Publishers, brokers, and customers are the three groups mentioned in the publish-subscribe model. Publishers provide data to brokers about subjects under their management. Consumers subscribe to topics, and brokers provide the consumers with data on those topics, as depicted in Figure 4-3. Therefore, it is the duty of brokers to receive data from publishers and transmit it to the proper consumer.

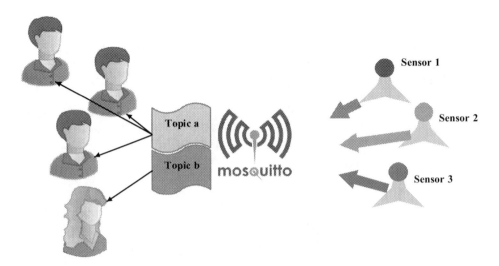

Figure 4-3. *Publish-subscribe model*

Push-Pull

Data consumers pull data from queues after data producers push data into them. Consumers and producers are not conversant with one another, as indicated in Figure 4-4. When producers produce data at a rate that is faster than the rate at which consumers can download it, queues serve as buffers.

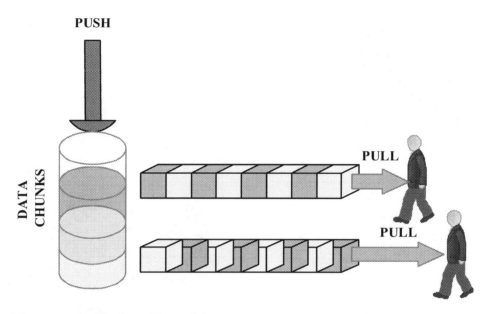

Figure 4-4. *Push-pull model*

Exclusive Pair

This model uses a persistent connection between the client and server and is a bidirectional, full-duplex communication architecture, as depicted in Figure 4-5. The connection is persistent and stays open until the client requests that it be closed. The server is aware of every open connection in this stateful connection paradigm.

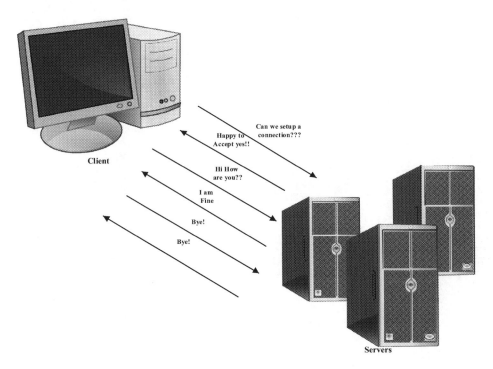

Figure 4-5. *Exclusive pair communication*

REST

For Representational State Transfer (REST) communication, the request-response model is used.

Components of the REST model are described in the following.

Client-server. Developers, based on requirement specification, increase the portability of the user interface across many platforms by separating the user interface concerns from the data storage problems and improve scalability by streamlining the server components. This indicates that since the server handles data storage, the client user interface shouldn't be bothered about it. This is similar to how the client handles the user interface; the server should not be bothered with it.

Each request from the client to the server must include all the information required to comprehend the request and cannot make use of any context that has been saved on the server. As a result, the client alone maintains the state of the session.

Data in response to a request must be explicitly or implicitly marked as cacheable or noncacheable to comply with cache limitations. If a response is cacheable, a client cache may use the response data for subsequent identical queries.

Uniform interfaces should be used for client-server communications. Each resource has a specific identifier, which is mentioned in the client requests. The client receives a representation of the resource based on the one they have requested. The client has the ability to alter this representation if server permits.

Layered system. By restricting component behavior so that each component may "see" only the immediate layer with which they are interacting, the layered system style enables an architecture to be made of hierarchical levels.

Code on demand (optional). REST enables the extension of client capabilities through the download and execution of scripts or applets. Because fewer functionalities need to be pre-implemented, the clients are simpler.

Resource. A resource is the primary information abstraction in REST. A document or image, a temporal service, a group of other resources, a nonvirtual entity (such a person), and other types of information that can be identified can all be considered resources. REST employs a resource identifier to pinpoint the specific resource involved in a component-component transaction.

The resource representation is the status of the resource at any given timestamp. Data, metadata that describes the data, and hypermedia linkages that can assist clients in moving to the next desirable state make up a representation.

Use these resource methods to carry out the necessary transformation.

IoT Levels: Templates for Deployment

IoT systems include the following elements:

- **Device**: These could be identification, remote sensing, or monitoring sensors or actuators.

- **Resources**: On IoT devices, these are software components for accessing, processing, storing, or controlling actuators connected to the device. Software parts that enable network connectivity are also resources. An application that runs on the device and communicates with web services is known as a *controller service*. The controller service uses web services to receive commands from the application and transfer data from the device to the web service to operate the device.

- **Databases**: Databases hold device-generated data. IoT devices, apps, databases, and analysis components are linked together through the use of web services.

- **Analysis component**: This analyzes the data produced by the IoT device and produces results in an understandable format for the user.

- **Application**: This offers a method for the user to check the system's status and see the data that has been processed. Additionally, it enables users to manage and keep an eye on many parts of the IoT system.

Levels of IoT

The levels of IoT are determined based on the number of nodes or devices dedicated for sensing, the location of updating the sensing information, the location of analytics of sensed data (local or remote), the mode of controlling and monitoring (local or remote), and the place of coordination. There are six levels of IoT as follows:

- **IoT level 1: IoT systems are comprised of a single node or device that carries out sensing or actuations, saves data, analyzes it, and hosts the application.**

   Consider an IoT device that keeps track of a home's lighting as an example. Switches are used to operate the lights. Each light's status is kept up-to-date in a local database. Locally installed REST services retrieve and update the status of every light in the database, which activates the switches accordingly. For locally controlling the lights or other applications, the application offers a user interface, as shown in Figure 4-6. The program can be viewed remotely because the device is linked to the Internet.

Figure 4-6. *Level 1 of IoT*

- **IoT level 2: A node performs sensing, actuation, and local analysis. The cloud is used to store data.**

  As an example, one node tracks the soil moisture in a field. Using REST APIs, this is transmitted to the cloud-based database, as shown in Figure 4-7. Moisture levels are regularly monitored by the controller service. The IoT system is monitored and managed using cloud-based software.

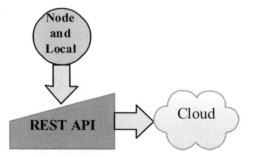

Figure 4-7. *Level 2 of IoT*

- **IoT level 3: A solitary node monitors the environment and uploads data to the cloud. An application runs in the cloud. This is appropriate in situations with large amounts of data and computationally expensive processing.**

  An example would be a node that uses a gyroscope and an accelerometer to monitor a package. These tools monitor vibration levels. Using the WebSocket API, the controller service transmits sensor data to the cloud in real time, as shown in Figure 4-8. A cloud-based application is used to visualize data that is stored in the cloud. When vibration levels reach a certain level, an analysis component sends out a warning.

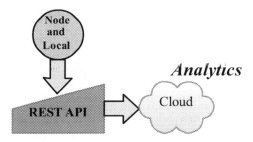

Figure 4-8. *Level 3 of IoT*

- **IoT level 4: Information is gathered by multiple nodes and stored in the cloud. The system is managed using a cloud-based application. There are present local and remote observer nodes that subscribe to and receive data gathered in the cloud from various devices. Observer nodes can analyze data and use it for applications, but they cannot exercise control.**

  An example would be the need for numerous nodes to operate independently when monitoring noise in an area. Everyone has a unique controller service. A cloud database is used to store data. The complete IoT system is monitored in the cloud via an application, and analysis is performed there as well.

- **IoT level 5: Nodes in the area fall into two categories: coordinator nodes and end nodes. End nodes gather information and carry out sensing, actuation, or both. Data from end nodes is gathered by coordinator nodes and sent to the cloud. Applications are cloud-based, and data is saved and analyzed there as well.**

The end nodes of a monitoring system, for instance, gather various types of environmental data and relay it to the coordination node, as shown in Figure 4-9. Data can be sent to cloud storage utilizing the REST API through the coordinator node, which serves as a gateway. Data is sent to the cloud by the controller service on the coordination node.

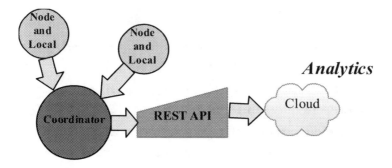

Figure 4-9.   *Level 5 of IoT*

- **IoT level 6: Several independent end nodes work together to transfer data to the cloud and perform sensing and actuation. Applications are cloud-based, and data is saved there as well. The data is analyzed by the analytics components, who then save the findings in a cloud database. An application built on the cloud is used to visualize the results. The centralized controller issues control directives to the end nodes while being aware of their current condition.**

As an example, sensors that monitor several characteristics of a system are used in weather monitoring. Data is sent to cloud storage by the end nodes. The storage, application, and analysis components are all in the cloud. A centralized controller provides inputs and regulates all nodes, as shown in Figure 4-10.

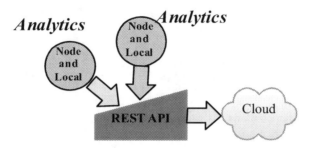

Figure 4-10.   *Level 6 of IoT*

Single-Board Computers and Internet of Things

A single-board computer (SBC) is a fully functional computer in which the CPU, input/output operations, memory, and other features are all integrated onto a single circuit board, with a fixed amount of RAM and no expansion slots for peripherals, as depicted in Figure 4-11. Single-board computers (SBCs), like the Raspberry Pi, are diminutive computers that can be used for a range of activities, including experimentation, learning how to program, prototypes building a media player or NAS drive, robotics, home automation, and simple computing tasks like web browsing or word processing. SBCs are being used more and more in a variety of industrial applications that involve AI and the IoT.

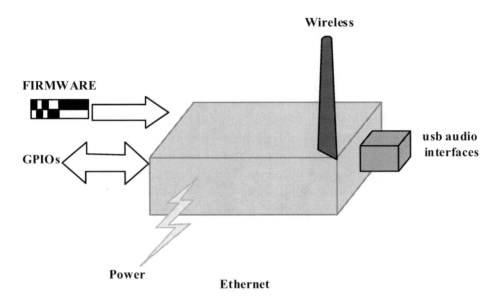

Figure 4-11. *Single-board computers used in IoT*

How to Choose a Single-Board Computer

When selecting an embedded processor for industrial applications, it is vital to understand the performance needs of the CPU. However, special attention should be made to incorporate a realistic assessment of the needed performance of the human-machine interface (HMI), especially for video, 2D graphics, and 3D graphics. Other factors, such as the peripheral mix, are also quite relevant. Once a performance requirement has been defined, applications can be loosely divided into three categories.

- **Less than 150 Dhrystone MIPS**: ARM Cortex-M3-based MCUs offer the best pricing and performance.

- **From 150 to 500 MIPS**: ARM9-based MPUs are likely to be the best option.

- **From 500 to 1,500 MIPS**: MPUs with a Cortex-A8 processor are ideal for more demanding computational tasks.

These are the principal subsystem elements:

- **Applications processor**: The OMAP processor series of multimedia application processors is ideally suited for these applications due to its exceptional computational capabilities. In addition, the highly integrated peripheral set has a large number of system-level components that will lower the overall bill of materials and PCB size. SmartReflex power and performance management solutions from TI decrease power usage by dynamically regulating voltage, frequency, and power according to device activity, modes of operation, and temperature.

- **SBC**: SBCs are tiny off-the-shelf motherboards with onboard I/Os. Because of their power density, low-power CPUs are nearly usually employed. The intended OMAP35x platform has essential characteristics such as:

  A Sitara ARM processor, which features Powerful ARM CortexTM-A8 up to 1GHz operation tuned for low-power consumption and a wide peripheral set consisting of UART, SPI, I2C, USB, and Ethernet

  Support for displays production-ready reference platforms

Support for TI-RTOS, Linux mainline, Android, and the Large 3P ecosystem

- The DSP-based video subsystem of the c64x+ (up to 720 HD resolution)

- Compatible OpenGL ES 2.0 graphics hardware (up to 10 M polygons per second)

- **HMI**: The usability of an HMI system is defined by its processing capacity, its ability to produce complex and reality-like screens, its quick response time to user input, and its adaptability to handle different levels of operator interactions. OMAP devices from Texas Instruments have the processing capability, graphical accelerators, and peripherals required to handle the expanding demands of the HMI market. OMAP's laptop-like computing performance enables the incorporation of new features and functionalities into any HMI without incurring excessive expenditures.

- **POS**: Texas Instruments provides processor systems with USB 2.0 and EMAC connection for the electronic point-of-service (POS) sector.

  - OMAP-L1x models incorporate an ARM9 at 300MHz and an optional floating or fixed DSP engine at 300MHz (total system performance of 600MHz), as well as the most peripherals in their category. Maximum 10mW standby power and 500mW running power. LCD and video support up to QVGA are the key features of this model.

- OMAP35x products have a typical operating power of 500mW and a standby power as low as 5mW. On these products, peripheral integration includes EMAC, CAN, USB OTG HS 2.0 PHY, 1.8V/3.3V IO, and LPDDR/DDR2 compatibility.

- **Connectivity**: Wireless connectivity to Bluetooth, WLAN, and 3G networks, as well as wired industry-standard communications such as CAN, UART, USB OTG, I2C, and 10/100 Mb Ethernet, are available. Depending on the needs of the final application, these interface options allow the system to be connected to a vast array of external peripherals and accessories.

- **Touch-screen controller**: TI's touch-screen controllers offer a low-power, high-performance solution that is well-suited to the touch-screen display's requirements. The controllers provide configurable resolution (8 or 12-bit), the control circuitry to measure touch pressure, and touch-screen measurement preprocessing to reduce bus loading, and hence lowering the use of host CPU resources, which can then be allocated to more important tasks.

Table 4-1 is a quick reference list that can help you choose the desired type from the available alternatives.

Table 4-1. *List of Battery Modules, Sensor Types, Single-Board Computers, and Wired and Wireless Communication Types*

Component	Types
Battery module	Zinc-air
	Lithium
	Lithium/Carbon mono-fluoride
	Alkaline
	Zinc-carbon
	Silver oxide
	Lithium thionyl chloride
	Lithium ion
	Lithium ion polymer
	Lithium manganese
	Lithium titanate
	Lithium phosphate
	Lithium cobalt
	Nickel cadmium
	Nickel-metal hydride
Sensor types	Active and Passive
	Noncontact and contact
	Relative and absolute
	Digital and analog

(*continued*)

Table 4-1. (*continued*)

Component	Types
Wired and wireless communication	I2C
	SPI
	UART
	USART
	RS485
	IPV4/V6
	Bacnet
	Bluetooth
	Wi-Fi
	ZigBee
	6LOWPAN
	RF
	Infrared
Single-board computers	Arduino
	ARM
	Asus
	Beaglebone
	Nvidia
	Raspberry Pi
	STM32

Available Single-Board Computers

Tables 4-2 to 4-6 provide the characteristics of 15 single-board computers. Figures 4-12 to 4-26 are the images of the 15 single-board computers discussed.

Table 4-2. *Features of Raspberry Pi 4B, Raspberry Pi 3A+, Raspberry Zero 2 W*

Name of Single-Board Computer	Raspberry Pi 4B	Raspberry Pi 3A+	Raspberry Zero 2 W
Architecture	ARM64 or 32	ARM64 or 32	ARM64 or 32
Clock speed	1.5GHz	1.4GHz	1GHz
RAM size available	1, 2, 3, 4, 8 GB	1 GB	512MB
Number of USB ports	2: USB 3.0	1: USB 2.0	1: USB 2.0
GPIOs	40	40	40
Connectivity	I2C, SPI, UART, ADC	I2C, SPI, UART, ADC	I2C, SPI, UART, ADC
Ethernet	Yes	No	No
Wi-Fi	Yes	Yes	Yes
Bluetooth	Yes	Yes	Yes
Operating system	Linux	Linux	Linux
Audio jack compatibility	Yes	Yes	No

Figure 4-12. *Raspberry Pi 4B*
Source: `https://robu.in/wp-content/uploads/2019/06/`
`Raspberry-Pi-4-4GB-Model-B-2.jpg`

Figure 4-13. *Raspberry Pi 3A+*
Source: `https://robu.in/wp-content/uploads/2018/11/`
`Raspberry-Pi-3-Model-A-1.jpg`

Figure 4-14. *Raspberry Pi Zero 2 W*
Source: *https://robu.in/wp-content/uploads/2021/10/rpi-zero.jpg*

Table 4-3. *Features of Raspberry Zero W, Raspberry Pi Pico,*
Raspberry Pi Pico W

Name of Single-Board Computer	Raspberry Zero W	Raspberry Pi Pico	Raspberry Pi Pico W
Architecture	ARM64	Arm Cortex M0+	Arm Cortex M0+
Clock speed	1GHz	133MHz	133MHz
RAM size available	512 MB	2 MB	2 MB
Number of USB ports	2: USB 2.0	Micro USB	Micro USB
GPIOs	40	26	26
Connectivity	I2C, SPI, UART, ADC.	SPI, UART, I2C, PWM	SPI, UART, I2C, PWM
Ethernet	No	No	No
Wi-Fi	Yes	No	Yes
Bluetooth	Yes	No	Yes
Operating system	Linux	NA	NA
Audio jack compatibility	No	No	No

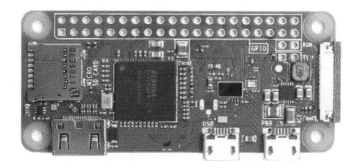

Figure 4-15. *Raspberry Pi Zero W*
Source: https://robu.in/wp-content/uploads/2020/07/
Raspberry-Pi-Zero-W-2-1.jpg

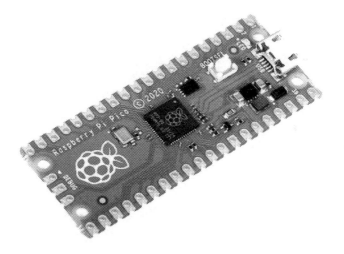

Figure 4-16. *Raspberry Pi Pico*
Source: https://robu.in/wp-content/uploads/2019/01/
Raspberry-PI-Pico-4.jpg

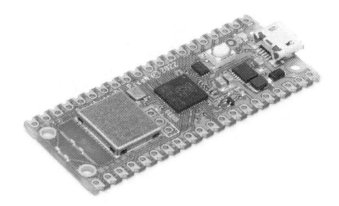

Figure 4-17. *Raspberry Pi Pico W*
Source: https://robu.in/wp-content/uploads/2022/06/
Raspberry-Pi-Pico-W_Raspberry-Pi-Boards-amp-Official-
Accessories_51556_1.png

Table 4-4. *Features of Rock 3A, Radxa Zero, Odyssey X86J4105*

Name of Single-Board Computer	Rock 3A	Radxa Zero	Odyssey X86J4105
Architecture	Quad-core Cortex-A55	Quad Cortex-A53	Intel® Celeron® J4105, Quad-Core
Clock speed	2GHz	1.8GHz	2.5GHz
RAM size available	2/4/8GB	4GB	8GB
Number of USB ports	1: USB 2.0, 2: USB 3.0	1: USB 2.0, 1: USB 3.0	2: USB 2.0, 2: USB 3.0
GPIOs	40	40	40
Connectivity	I2C, SPI, UART, ADC, CAN, PWM.	I2C, SPI, UART, ADC, CAN, PWM, SPDIF	I2C, SPI, UART, ADC, CAN, PWM, SPDIF

(continued)

Table 4-4. (*continued*)

Ethernet	Yes	No	Yes
Wi-Fi	Yes	Yes	Yes
Bluetooth	Yes	Yes	Yes
Operating system	Android 11.0, Debian 10/ Ubuntu/ Slackware	Android 11.0, Debian 10/Ubuntu/Linux-based systems	Linux
Audio jack compatibility	Yes	No	Yes

Figure 4-18. *Rock 3A*

Figure 4-19. *Radxa Zero*

Figure 4-20. *Odyssey X86J4105*
Source: https://robu.in/wp-content/uploads/2020/04/13.jpg

Table 4-5. *Features of Vision Five, Nezha, Odroid C4*

Name of Single-Board Computer	Vision Five	Nezha	Odroid C4
Architecture	StarFive JH71I0 64bit	XuanTie C906 64-bit RISC-V processor	quad-core Cortex-A55
Clock speed	1.5GHz	1.0GHz	2.0GHz
RAM size available	2/4/8GB	1GB	4GB
Number of USB	2: USB 2.0, 2 to USB 3.0	2: USB 2.0	4: USB 3.0
GPIOs	40	40	40
Connectivity	I2C, SPI, UART, ADC, CAN, PWM, SPDIF	I2C, SPI, UART, ADC, CAN, PWM, SPDIF	I2C, SPI, UART, ADC, CAN
Ethernet	Yes	Yes	Yes
Wi-Fi	Yes	Yes	Yes
Bluetooth	Yes	Yes	Yes
Operating system	Linux	Linux	Linux
Audio jack compatibility	Yes	Yes	No

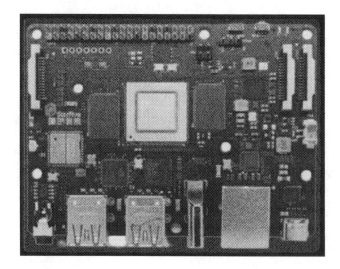

Figure 4-21. *Vision five*

Figure 4-22. *Nezha*

Figure 4-23. *Odroid C4*

Table 4-6. *Features of LattePanda, Tinkerboard, NVIDIA Jetson Nano*

Name of Single-Board Computer	LattePanda	Tinker Board	NVIDIA Jetson Nano
Architecture	Atom-based x86	Quad-core ARM-based	Quad core ARM SoM
Clock speed	3.4GHz	600MHz	
RAM size available	8GB	2GB	4GB
Number of USB ports	2: USB 3.0	2: USB 3.0	4: USB 3.0
GPIOs	40	40	40
Connectivity	I2C, SPI, UART, ADC, CAN, PWM, SPDIF	I2C, SPI, UART, ADC, CAN, PWM, SPDIF	I2C, SPI, UART, ADC, CAN, PWM, SPDIF
Ethernet	Yes	Yes	Yes

(continued)

Table 4-6. (*continued*)

Wi-Fi	Yes	Yes	No
Bluetooth	Yes	Yes	No
Operating system	Windows	Linux	Linux
Audio jack compatibility	Yes	Yes	Yes

Figure 4-24. *LattePanda*
Source: https://robu.in/wp-content/uploads/2022/08/
LattePanda-V1-4GB64GB-with-Enterprise-License-1.jpg

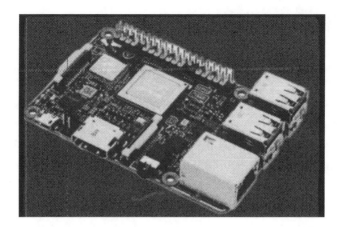

Figure 4-25. *TinkerBoard*

Figure 4-26. *NVIDIA Jetson Nano*
Source: https://robu.in/wp-content/uploads/2019/12/jet.jpg

Summary

This chapter discussed the benefits of the IoT in business processes, various levels of IoT, and how to select a single-board computer for your application. Finally, we discussed 15 single-board computers along with their features to help you choose the best board for your application. The next chapter provides you with insights into how an application can be monitored and controlled visually with the help of dashboards.

CHAPTER 5

Introduction to Dashboards

A *dashboard* is a tool to monitor and analyze the activities or events of the organization. It helps top-level employees and business partners gain knowledge about all department activities and their well-being, ranging from macro- to micro-level processes. The visual information displayed on the dashboard is used to make major decisions about crucial issues behind the scenes. It links various metrics with each process or activity and extracts suitable data or information for displaying the data visually in an easily understandable manner.

This chapter covers how to install the Dash library with a simple program, the Dash HTML components, the core Dash components, and various graphs such as pie charts, choropleth maps, bubble charts, and funnel charts.

Data Dashboards

Data dashboards help executive officers understand the overall performance of their organization or industry along with where improvement or special attention is necessary. Data dashboards are designed to contribute to business intelligence and support the continuous success of the business.

© G.R. Kanagachidambaresan, Bharathi N. 2023
G.R. Kanagachidambaresan and N. Bharathi, *Sensors and Protocols for Industry 4.0*,
Maker Innovations Series, https://doi.org/10.1007/978-1-4842-9007-1_5

The Dash library is open-source and can be used to design more powerful and appealing dashboards in Python. Dash was released by the Plotly company, which also developed and released the Plotly data visualization library in Python. The added benefit is that the Dash library can be easily integrated with the Plotly library to support the design of data-oriented dashboards. Although you can create a dashboard easily with the Dash library, integrating the dashboards with web-based applications is achieved with Flask and React. Flask is a framework based on the REST API for web applications developed by Armin Ronacher in Python. React is a JavaScript-based web application library for building rich user interfaces to run in browsers. Companies using Flask are Netflix, Reddit, Lyft, and more. Companies using React are Airbnb, Uber, Facebook, and more.

Dash is more useful for data scientists who handle the data in a more intelligent way to gain insights from it and share it with executives and businesspeople for decision-making. Dash can be used to create dashboards for a range of domains such as finance and marketing, healthcare and diagnostics, supply chain and inventory, etc. Dash supports the development of simple data visualization dashboards to more sophisticated interactive dashboards. The examples you'll see in this chapter show the various dashboards and their components that can be used for industries adopting Industry 4.0.

The Dash library is implemented on Plotly.js and React.js to develop and deploy elegant data dashboards with custom-made user interfaces for any kind of application. It precisely supports almost all advanced algorithms, techniques, and protocols for the development of full-stack web applications. The Dash library can be installed appropriately in any Python IDE, and simple dashboards can be developed in less than 30 minutes.

Installing Dash

In the Python terminal, type the following command to install Dash:

```
pip install dash
```

If you are using Jupyter Notebook, enter the following command:

```
pip install jupyter-dash
```

Along with Dash, the Pandas library is necessary to handle datasets and can be installed as follows:

```
pip install pandas
```

The Basic Code

After you've installed the necessary libraries, your first new code can be typed in the editor or in Jupyter Notebook as follows:

```
from dash import Dash, dcc, html
import plotly.express as px
import pandas as pd
```

The Plotly Express libraries are easy to use and include functions for graphs, plots, charts, maps, etc. It is also required for building data dashboards and can be imported as follows along with other necessary components such as Dash and Pandas:

```
app = Dash(title = 'Dash - Illustration')
```

Dash() provides the environment to build a systematic web application. It has more than 25 parameters for configuring the web application. Among them, the title parameter displays the title of the web page, and the server parameter, which is True by default, sets up the server for the web application using Flask. The dash() call returns an app instance in which dashboard components can be added with the layout() method.

You can create a sample dataset with a set of sensors that is used in agriculture and the supply chain industry using Python code with the Pandas library. The dataset can also be read from the CSV file using the read_csv() function in the Pandas library.

```
df = pd.DataFrame({
    "Sensors": ["Temperature", "pressure", "Humidity",
    "Temperature", "pressure", "Humidity"],
    "Count": [45, 54, 33, 22, 14, 31],
    "Industry": ["Agriculture", "Agriculture", "Agriculture",
    "Supplychain", "Supplychain", "Supplychain"]
})
```

This program builds a dashboard, for example, with a bar chart depicting the sensor types and their corresponding counts used in agriculture and the supply chain industry. The code is organized to display a heading, a paragraph, and a bar chart. The chart is created using the Plotly Express object px and the function bar(). This function takes nearly 42 parameters or arguments in terms of key-value pairs. Every argument has its purpose to fine-tune the bar chart. The minimum required parameters are added in the following function call to display the bars in the chart. They are the x dimension of the chart, which is a series or array; the y dimension, which is also a series or array; the color of the bars, which is specified by the values in a particular column; and the barmode setting to arrange the bars.

```
chart = px.bar(df, x="Sensors", y= "Count", color= "Industry",
barmode="group")
```

In this code, the x key is assigned to the list of sensors, and the y key is assigned to the list of its count. The color is decided based on agriculture or the supply chain. The barmode has three values: relative, overlay, and group. In relative mode, the bars are stacked either in positive or negative dimensions based on their values. In overlay mode, the bars are displayed one on top of another. In group mode, the bars are placed side-by-side. Finally, the chart needs to be positioned properly in the web page based on its layout.

The layout of the page is designed using the Dash HTML components. Many HTML components exist to properly display the components on the web page. In this example dashboard, only Div, H1, and P are used. Div() is the wrapper function for the div tag in HTML. The div tag in HTML is a general container for organizing its content with the stylesheet. As it is called a *container*, the children key is one of the arguments, or parameters, and the heading H1() and paragraph P() functions are the values of the children key of Div(). In addition, one of the core Dash components, Graph(), is also the value of the child key of Div(). The Graph() function from the core Dash component (dcc) also has arguments as a key-value pair. Two keys called id and figure are used for the unique identification of the graph and what needs to be displayed in the graph, respectively.

```
app.layout = html.Div(children=[
    html.H1(children='Data Dashboard'),
    html.P('Dash: A web application framework for data
    visualization'),
    dcc.Graph( id='first-graph', figure=chart)
    ])
```

The core Dash components library has several functions, such as Graph() for customizing the data dashboards to suit the industry needs. The Graph() function has several parameters. Among them is id for uniquely identifying this graph and a figure parameter for displaying the graph or chart, which is of the Plotly object. In this example, the Plotly object is a chart that depicts the bar chart. Further details about the

Graph() function can be obtained from https://dash.plotly.com/dash-core-components/graph. Finally, the web page building part is completed with the close brackets for the Div() function.

```
if __name__ == '__main__':
    app.run_server(debug=True, use_reloader=False)
app.run_server(host='127.0.0.1', port='8050', proxy=None,
debug=True, dev_tools_ui=None, ......)
```

The Flask server is started using the function call run_server() with the Dash object app. The host argument specifies the IP address for serving the application as a server. This run_server() call is for the local development mode, and the deployment in production can use gunicorn(unix)/waitress(windows). The port argument by default is 8050, but it can also be assigned with other values. The next argument proxy is by default none. The debug argument, if it is set to True, enables all the dev tools, which helps in tracking the errors during development in the browser. The use-reloader set to False ensures that only one instance of the Flask server is running because in debug mode, any change in the code automatically forks its child.

Dash is running on http://127.0.0.1:8050/.

```
* Serving Flask app "__main__" (lazy loading)
* Environment: production
  WARNING: This is a development server. Do not use it in a
  production deployment.
  Use a production WSGI server instead.
* Debug mode: on
```

The previous information is displayed if the Flask app server starts running. Obviously, the warning message insists that this code should be executed in local development mode and not for the production server. The previous code segment generates the dashboard shown in Figure 5-1.

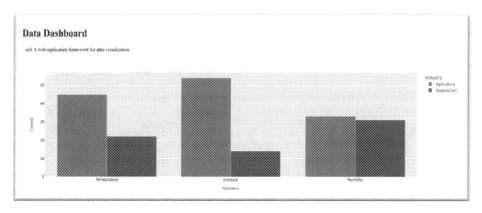

Figure 5-1. *Data dashboard using a bar chart*

Dash HTML Components

Generally, the HTML documents are built with html tags and formatted using style sheets. Simple static web pages are displayed with HTML documents. The following is an HTML document that displays a web page, as shown in Figure 5-2. These simple web pages and interactive dashboards can be created with Dash HTML components and Dash core components.

```
<div>
    <h1>Dash-HTML Demonstration</h1>
    <br>
    <div>
        <p>Python paragraph function is displaying as <p> in
        html </p>
        <p> The conversion of python functions into
        corresponding HTML tag happens during execution by
        dash-html-component </p>
    </div>
</div>
```

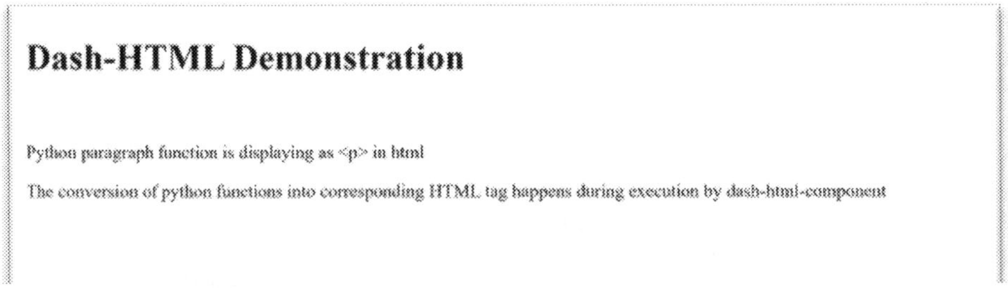

Dash-HTML Demonstration

Python paragraph function is displaying as <p> in html

The conversion of python functions into corresponding HTML tag happens during execution by dash-html-component

Figure 5-2. HTML heading, paragraph, and line break using Dash

The dashboard arrangement, when the page is loaded in the web browser, is accomplished with the Dash component assigned to the app layout. A function call that returns the Dash component can also be assigned to it. In this example, the html.Div() function call is used, which returns the Dash HTML component and is assigned to app.layout. html.Div() is a wrapper for the div tag in HTML. It serves as a container for other components. It has several arguments, such as children, id, etc., which can be passed in the function call to configure the container and its components. The following code segment, which is implemented with Python in Dash, displays the same dashboard as the previous HTML document:

```
app.layout = html.Div([
    html.H1('Dash-HTML Demonstration'),
    html.Br(),
    html.Div([
        html.P('Python paragraph function is displaying as <p>
        in html'),
        vhtml.P('The conversion of python functions into
        corresponding HTML tag happens during execution by
        dash-html-component')
    ])
])
```

HTML Heading

The layout comprises an HTML heading with an H1() function call. This function displays a heading that is passed as the children argument. Many other arguments also exist, such as id, title, style, etc., for provisioning the heading with more features. This function serves as a wrapper for the <H1> tag in HTML. Similarly, other heading function calls also exist. They are dash.html.H2(), dash.html.H3(), dash.html.H4(), dash.html.H5(), and dash.html.H6().

HTML Break

The function called html.Br() is a wrapper of the br tag in HTML. It creates a line break in the web page. The content following this function call will be displayed on the next line. A line break is generally used to divide the contents of the page in a meaningful and understandable way.

HTML Paragraph

The HTML paragraphs are used to display the text-based documents on web pages. The blocks of text are separated using the p tag in HTML. In this example, the htmlP() function displays paragraphs and serves as a wrapper for the p tag. The html.P() function has several arguments that are used for formatting the paragraphs while displayed on the dashboard.

HTML Images

HTML pages support figures, and their wrappers are implemented with Dash HTML components. Html.Figure() is a container to hold an image and its caption with html.Img() and html.Figcaption(). Html.Img() is used to display an image by assigning the location of the image file to the source src attribute. The caption to the image can be added suitably with html.Figcaption() and its children attribute. In this example, the figure caption is enclosed in bold font using the html.B() function and is displayed in the dashboard as shown in Figure 5-3.

```
html.Div([
        html.Br(),
        html.Figure(title = 'Dash-HTML Figure wrapper
        component', children = [
            html.B([
            html.Figcaption( children = 'Dash-HTML-Figure
            demonstration')]),
            html.Img(src='https://www.gizelis.com/images/
            industry4/industry4.0.jpg')])
    ])
```

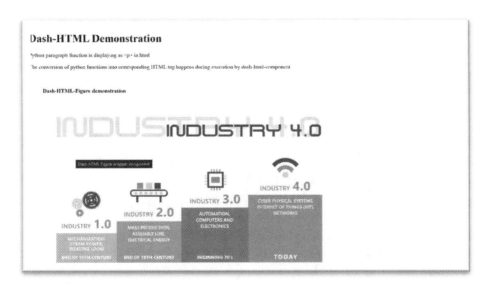

Figure 5-3. *HTML figure, figure caption, and image using Dash*

The figure caption can be located either above the image or below the image by calling html.Img() and html.Figcaption() accordingly. In the following code, the figure caption function is called after the image to display the image "Industry 4.0." In addition, a title has been added for html.Figure(), which displays the text as a tooltip when the mouse pointer moves over the figure component. Additionally, the style argument is added to html.Img() to specify the width and height of the image, and the corresponding dashboard is demonstrated in Figure 5-4.

```
html.Figure(title = 'Dash-HTML Figure wrapper component',
children = [
          html.Img(src='https://www.gizelis.com/images/
          industry4/industry4.0.jpg',
           style={'width': 300, 'height': 200})]),
          html.B([
             html.Figcaption( children = 'Dash-HTML-Figure
             demonstration')]),
```

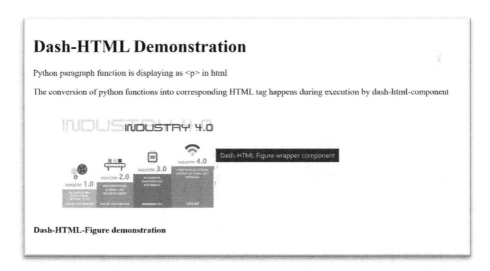

Figure 5-4. *Style for size of image and placement of figure caption below the image*

HTML Label

The purpose of each component in the HTML document is described
by a label tag. The corresponding wrapper for the label tag is html.
Label(). In this example, it is added inside the figure container and above
the image to display the text "Dash-HTML-Label Component" with the
color attribute in the style argument set to red. Figure 5-5 shows the
corresponding dashboard.

```
html.Figure(title = 'Dash-HTML Figure wrapper component',
children = [
          html.B([html.Label(style = {'color': 'red'},
          children = 'Dash-HTML-Label Component')]),
          html.Br(),
          html.Img(src='https://www.gizelis.com/images/
          industry4/industry4.0.jpg', style={'width': 300,
          'height': 200})])
```

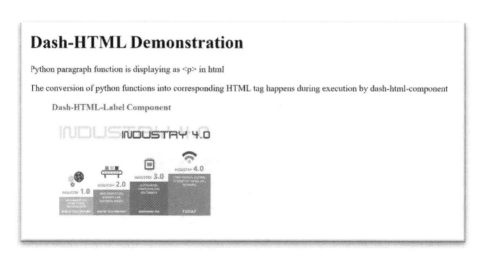

Figure 5-5. *HTML label in red using Dash*

Dash Core Components

The core components in Dash are included in the dashboard by importing the dash.dcc library using the Python statement from dash import dcc. The dcc library has various components, such as check boxes, radio buttons, drop-down boxes, sliders, range sliders, text boxes, and text areas, that can be used to create attractive and interactive dashboards.

Checklists

Check boxes are grouped under a category and used to select more than one item from that category. The dashed core component is dcc. The checklist() method is used to create a group of check boxes with its mandatory arguments options and value. The options can be specified in various ways. The simplest way is to pass the Python list for both arguments. The options argument specifies the set of all check boxes needed to be displayed in the dashboard. The value argument specifies the subset of check boxes that are selected when the web-based dashboard is loaded and displayed.

```
from dash import dcc
...........
...........
app.layout = html.Div([
        html.H1("Demonstration of Check boxes"),
        html.Br(),
            dcc.Checklist(options=['Raspberry Pi', 'Beagle
            Bone', 'Intel Galileo'],
                                    value = ['Raspberry Pi'])
])
............
```

In this example, processor board names such as Raspberry Pi, Beagle Bone, and Intel Galileo are included as check box options with the Raspberry Pi in the selected state using a value argument while loading the dashboard, as shown in Figure 5-6.

Figure 5-6. *Demonstration of Dash core component: checklist*

Drop-Downs

A drop-down list is also used for grouping a set of elements under a single category, and one or multiple items can be selected. The main difference between a check box and a drop-down is the space optimization in the dashboard. The checklist displays all the elements in its category, and each is prefixed with a check box. By contrast, a drop-down displays only one element or a general string that describes the drop-down with a downward arrow on the right. If the arrow is clicked, all the elements in the drop-down are displayed.

```
app.layout = html.Div([
       html.H1("Demonstration of Dropdown box"),
       html.Br(),
       dcc.Dropdown(options=['Raspberry Pi', 'Beagle Bone',
       'Intel Galileo'],
                    value = ['Raspberry Pi'],
                 style = {'helght':300, 'width':300})
                 ])
```

In this example, the same set of processor boards is added in the drop-down `options` argument. The Raspberry Pi board is selected to be displayed in the dashboard while loading using a `value` argument. Click the down arrow as shown in Figure 5-7 to view all the options in the drop-down.

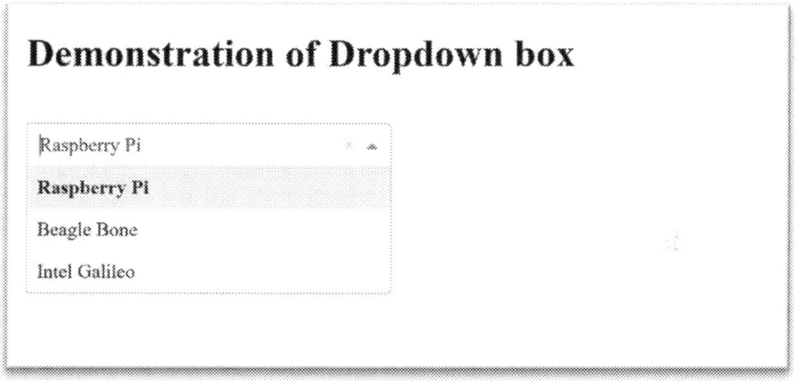

Figure 5-7. *Demonstration of the Dash core component: a drop-down box*

Radio Items

Radio buttons are grouped under a category and collectively called *radio items* in Dash core components. Unlike a checklist, only one option can be chosen from the set of radio items. In this component, the arguments are also `options` and `value`. To demonstrate the code block for adding radio items in the dashboard, this example uses the same `options` and `value` as in the previous checklist and drop-down examples. Figure 5-8 shows the resulting dashboard.

```
app.layout = html.Div([
        html.H1("Demonstration of Radio Items"),
        html.Br(),
```

```
        dcc.RadioItems(options=['Raspberry Pi', 'Beagle Bone',
    'Intel Galileo'],
                    value = ['Raspberry Pi'])
])
```

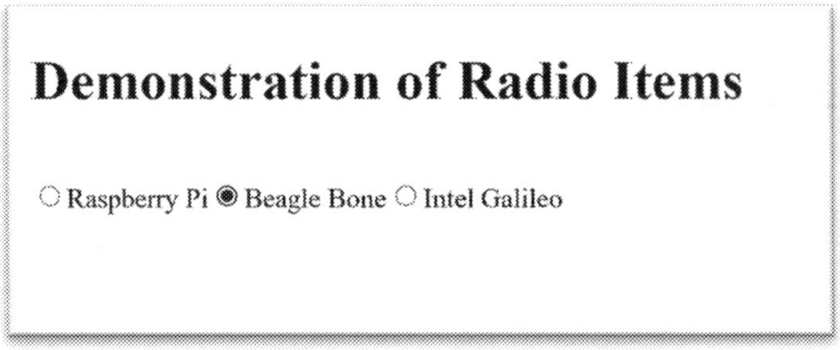

Demonstration of Radio Items

○ Raspberry Pi ● Beagle Bone ○ Intel Galileo

Figure 5-8. *Demonstration of core Dash component: radio items*

Sliders

The slider component allows us to select a value along the scrolling bar. The settings such as volume, brightness, and even color palette for images, etc., are adjusted by the slider. One end of the slide has a minimum allowable value, and the other end has a maximum allowable value. As the handle in the slider moves, the corresponding feature changes gradually in its value.

```
app.layout = html.Div(children = [
            html.H1("Demonstration of Slider"),
            html.Br(),
            html.Div(style = {'helght':300,
            'width':300,'background':  'white' 'margin-left':
            '15px', 'font-size':'large','font-weight':'bold'},
                    children = [dcc.Slider(10, 50, 5,
                        value=10,
                        id='slider-demo')])
    ])
```

In this example, the call to the method dcc.Slider() results in the slider, as displayed in Figure 5-9. The first three arguments denote the minimum, maximum, and step values, and their positions are fixed in the first three positions if the keywords min, max, and step are not used. The rest of the arguments, such as value, id, etc., can be specified using the respective keys. Marks along the slider are autogenerated by default and can be turned off if not needed. Marks can also be specified as custom marks by setting the key step = Null. The slider can also be placed in the vertical direction by setting the vertical key to True. Many other arguments exist to customize the slider in our own way.

Demonstration of Slider

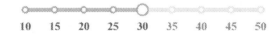

Figure 5-9. *Demonstration of the core Dash component: slider*

Range Sliders

The range slider is used to select a lesser range of values from the larger range. It has a double handle that is used to expand or shrink the selected subrange. The first three arguments are positional arguments to specify the minimum, maximum, and step. The keywords min, max, and step can also be used to specify the three arguments. Other arguments, such as value, which is a two-element list, specify the selected range and the ID with which RangeSlider can be accessed.

```
app.layout = html.Div(children = [
              html.H1("Demonstration of Slider"),
              html.Br(),
              html.Div(style = {'helght':300,
              'width':500,'background': 'white', 'margin-
              left': '15px', 'font-size':'large'},
                       children = [html.B(dcc.
                       RangeSlider(10, 50, 2,
                          value=[20,30],
                          id='RangeSlider-demo'))])
    ])
```

In this example, the dcc.RangeSlider() method is called with a minimum of 10, a maximum of 50, and a step of 2. In addition, the two-element list [20,30] is assigned to the value key for selecting that subrange, while the dashboard contains this RangeSlider to display, as shown in Figure 5-10. Additionally, in both Slider and RangeSlider, the style key of the html.Div() method, which holds RangeSlider or Slider, is set for its height, width, background, and margin-left.

Demonstration of Range Slider

Figure 5-10. *Demonstration of the core Dash component: range slider*

Input (Text Boxes)

The design of dashboards is not fulfilled if there is no provision for text-based input. The dcc.Input() method is provided for collecting user input as simple text in a single line. The notable argument in this method

164

is debounce. If debounce is set to True, the changes made to the input will be notified after the user presses Enter or when the input loses focus. Alternatively, if it is set to False, each and every change to the input is notified to its listener or callback() method immediately, and by default, it is set to False.

```
app.layout = html.Div(style = {'helght':500,
'width':500,'background': 'pink'},
        children = [
        html.H1("Demonstration of Input TextBox"),
        html.Br(),
        dcc.Input(id = 'inputtext',type = 'text'),
        html.B(html.Div(style = {'background':
        'lightblue','color': 'Magenta'},id='output'))
        ])

@app.callback(
    Output('output','children'),
    Input('inputtext', 'value')
)
def update_output(input1):
    return 'you have entered:-     "' + format(input1)+ '"'
```

In this example demonstration, the input core component is included in the dashboard to obtain text inputs. The type key, or argument, can be set to number to accept only numeric values. The other possible values for the type key are password, email, URL, etc. The html.Div() call is made to display the text, which is typed in the text box and enclosed in html.B() to make the text bold. Whatever the user is typing in the input text box will appear in the next section as simple text with the "you have entered:-" prefix. The user entered *This is Input Demo*, as displayed in Figure 5-11. Additionally, the background and text color are set to light blue and magenta, respectively, using a style key.

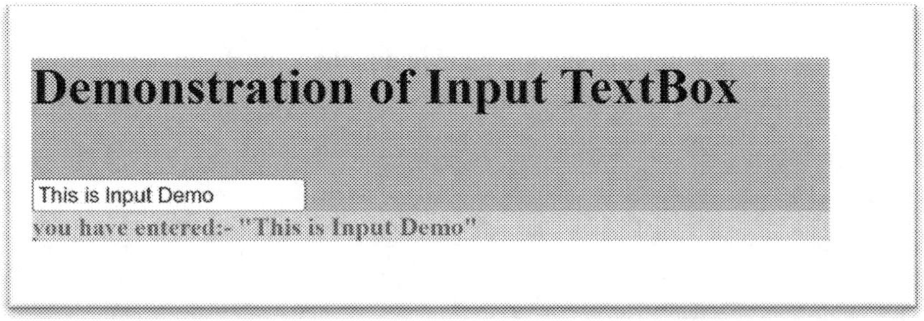

Figure 5-11. *Demonstration of dcc components: input*

Callbacks

The interactive dashboards can be developed using `callback()` functions. Every action of the user on the dashboard can be treated as input, such as entering the characters in input, clicking any component, moving the mouse over the component, dragging the component, etc. Those inputs are captured using `callback()` functions as input. The change or action on input is notified to the core `dcc` or `html` component, which is listening constantly as output. The `callback()` is a Python decorator that encloses another function for updating the dashboard based on any user actions or events and hence is used for interactive dashboards.

Input and Output in Callbacks

The `callback()` function has one or more outputs followed by one or more inputs as its syntax. The input argument of `callback()` tracks the particular component actions specified by its ID and value or any other key of that component. `def update_output(inputs...)` holds the processing part applied on input and returned to the output `callback()`. Output `callback()` obtains the value returned from the `update_output()` method and assigns it to children in its argument list. The very important rule that needs to be followed is the order of input callbacks, and the order of output callbacks should match the order of inputs passed to update_ output(inputs...) and return values. In the previous example, the input text box component is passed inputtext as its ID to the input callback() function. Additionally, the return value is assigned to the children of the html.Div component. The following code block illustrates the general syntax of callback:

```
@app.callback(
    Output('id of output','children'),
    Input('id of input', 'value')
)
def function_name(input1)
        #processing
        return 'output1'
```

Text Areas

The text area is required as the input component if the text input is more than one line of text. It is widely used for collecting reviews, suggestions, comments, recommendations, etc. The text entered in the text area can be processed by text processing applications, and the review or comment can be classified as positive or negative. The rows and columns arguments of the dcc.Textarea() method determine the size of the text area. The Autofocus argument is set to True to blink the cursor on the text area when the page is loaded. The minimum and maximum numbers of characters are specified using minLength and maxLength arguments, respectively. The text area can be set as the required field when submitting forms with the required argument of type Boolean. The text direction can be set either from left to right or from right to left.

```
app.layout = html.Div(style = {'helght':500,
'width':500,'background': 'pink'},
```

```
        children = [
        html.H1("Demonstration of Text Area"),
        html.Br(),
        dcc.Textarea(id = 'TA',rows = 3),
        html.B(html.Div(style = {'background':
        'lightblue','color': 'Magenta'},id='output'))
        ])
@app.callback(
    Output('output','children'),
    Input('TA', 'value')
)
def update_output(input1):
    return 'you have entered:-    "' + format(input1)+ '"'
```

In this example, the text area is configured with three rows of text with the ID TA. Similar to the input text box demonstration in the previous example, the content of the text area is displayed in the next section of the dashboard when it changes, as shown in Figure 5-12.

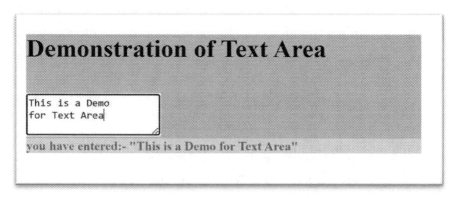

Figure 5-12. *Demonstration of dcc components: text area*

Putting It All Together

The following example code demonstrates the usage of checklists, radio items, drop-downs, sliders, and range sliders for the `ford.csv` dataset from Kaggle. The CSV file is copied in the data frame `cars` using the following code:

```
cars = pd.read_csv('ford.csv')
```

The various models are listed as checklists. The transmission of the model is configured as radio items. The year of model release is enumerated in a drop-down. The price range of all models is shown using a slider, and finally, the range of engine sizes of the car models is numbered using a range slider. The additional dashboard display configuration included in this example is an arrangement of components in a row or column. It is achieved by stating the `column` or `row` value for the `flex-direction` key of the style argument of the `html.Div()` method. The corresponding dashboard is displayed in Figure 5-13, in which the checklist and radio items belonging to the same `html.Div()` are arranged in a row, and other components that belong to the next section are arranged in a single column one after the other.

```
html.Br(),
html.Div(style = {'background':'pink','padding': 10, 'flex':
1}, children = [
            html.B([html.Label('Price Range of Cars', style
            = {'text-align': 'center'}),
            dcc.Slider(cars['price'].min(),cars['price'].
            max(),1000, value = 100)])
            ]),
        html.Br(),
        html.Div(style = {'background':'lightpink','padding
        ': 10, 'flex':1}, children = [
```

```
          html.B([html.Label('Engine size of Cars', style
          = {'text-align': 'center'}),
          dcc.RangeSlider(cars['engineSize'].
          min(),cars['engineSize'].max(),0.5,
                  value = [cars['engineSize'].
                  mean()-0.5,cars['engineSize'].
                  mean()+0.5])])
          ]),
     ]),
  ])
```

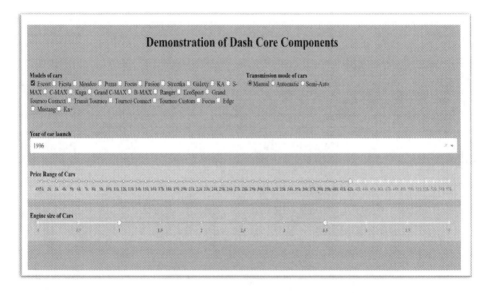

Figure 5-13. _Core components for single dataset visualization_

Graphs

The graph component in the dcc library encloses any type of chart generated with Plotly Express. Graphs have a major role in dashboards. They support data visualization in different ways, and not all types of charts are suitable for all kinds of data. The goodness of dashboards in all perspectives lies in the selection of suitable charts for the data in hand. The following charts give you the basic approach of selecting charts.

Pie Charts

The pie charts are useful when percentage data needs to be displayed in which the entire circle denotes 100 percent. They are especially suitable for comparing the various partitions or parts of a single concept or object. Generally, people can understand the contribution of various sources for a single outcome using pie charts.

```
import dash
from dash import html
from dash import dcc
import pandas as pd
import plotly.express as px
Fordcars = pd.read_csv('ford.csv')    # taken from Kaggle
car_options = [{'label':i,'value':i} for i in
Fordcars['model'].unique()]
pie_fig = px.pie(Fordcars, values = 'tax',names = 'model',title
= 'model-tax', width = 700, height = 700)
app.layout = html.Div([html.H1('Ford cars Analytics
Dashboard'),
                        dcc.Graph(figure = pie_fig)
                        ])
if(__name__)=='__main__':
    app.run_server(port=8052, debug=True, use_reloader=False)
```

In this example, the ford.csv dataset from Kaggle is used to demonstrate the pie chart in Figure 5-14. The tax for each model of Ford cars is represented as a percentage. This clearly shows which model has the highest tax and which model has the lowest tax. Additionally, other model taxes and their percentages can be analyzed at a glance. The pie chart was generated with the `px.pie()` method in the Plotly Express library. It takes the entire data frame as its first argument, and the columns that need to be visualized as `pie` should be passed in a value argument with its label (here it is the Ford car model name) in the `names` argument. Many more arguments exist to customize the chart in a desired and attractive way. The pie chart displayed in Figure 5-14 shows all models and their taxes collectively for 100 percent.

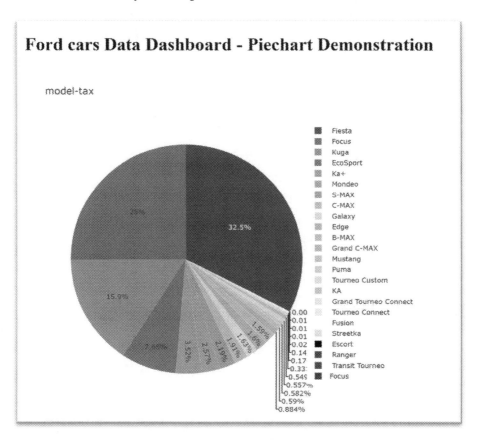

Figure 5-14. *Pie chart using the Ford car dataset*

The four pie charts in Figure 5-15 are generated by selecting the first six models and six successive models in the same pie chart displayed as a whole in Figure 5-14. The flexibility of viewing selected models and analyzing their contribution alone is also possible without separately coding for it. Selecting new models will generate new pie charts of only the selected models and their tax percentage as a whole.

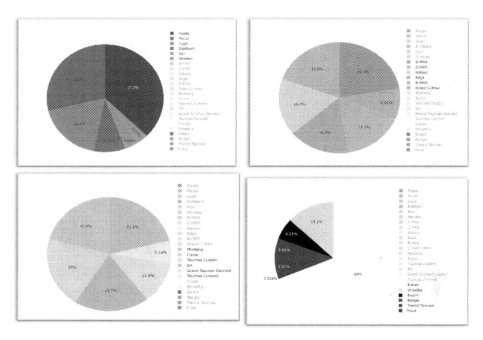

Figure 5-15. *Six car models selected in four groups and their tax analysis*

Choropleth Maps

Many business dashboards use choropleth maps to study the international status of their business visually with geographical maps. The worldwide branches of business, profits, popularity of products, sudden demand for products, shipment of products, etc., can be studied using these kinds of maps.

```
df = pd.read_csv("population_by_country_2020.csv")
# from kaggle

Population= px.choropleth(df, locations='Country', locationmode
= 'country names',
                                color='Population (2020)',  color_
                                continuous_scale="reds",
                                scope="world" )
urbanPop = px.choropleth(df, locations='Country', locationmode
= 'country names',
color='Urban Pop %', color_continuous_scale="magenta",
                                scope="world" )
app.layout = html.Div(style = {'width' :1200}, children =
[html.H1('World population Dashboard'),
                                dcc.Graph(figure = Population),
                                dcc.Graph(figure = urbanPop)
        ])
```

In the example code block, a choropleth map is generated with world population data from 2020.

The world population is depicted in Figure 5-16, with the population distribution percentage in urban areas in each country. The scope argument and the locationmode argument hold the geographical information of the map. The location and color arguments specify the data from the dataset to generate the choropleth map.

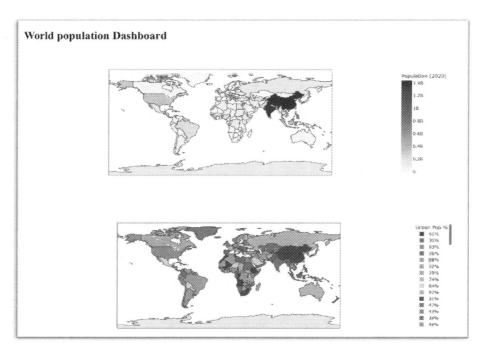

Figure 5-16. *World population (number) and urban population (%)*

Bubble Charts

Bubble charts are suitable for diverse ranges and scattered data. Data
that has no pattern and is distributed over a large range can be analyzed
using a bubble chart. The px.scatter() method generates the chart with
x and y arguments as the amount of data, and color and size arguments
specify the nature of the data in the dataset by varying accordingly. The
hover_name argument displays the information about the data point when
the mouse is moved over it.

```
df = pd.read_csv("population_by_country_2020.csv")
LandArea = px.scatter(df, x = np.random.rand(235), y=np.random.
rand(235),size='Land Area (sq.Km)',  color='Land Area (sq.
Km)',hover_name='Country')
```

175

```
app.layout = html.Div(style = {'width' :1200}, children =
[html.H1('World LandArea Dashboard'),
      dcc.Graph(figure = LandArea),
  ])
```

The example code segment demonstrates a bubble chart by mapping the land area of the countries in different sizes and color to display the variation, as shown in Figure 5-17. The land area of Russia is bigger, and hence the bubble is in yellow, but it has a very small dot to specify the population is less than India and China, which have larger bubbles.

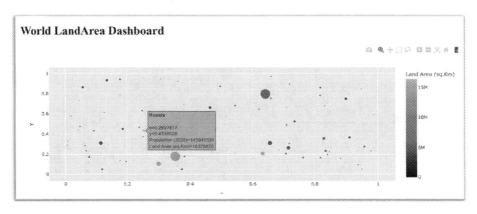

Figure 5-17. *Bubble chart: population by size and land area by color scale*

Funnel Charts

The progress of any process or any action can be displayed using a funnel chart. The funnel chart function in Plotly Express is specified as px. funnel(). The first argument is the data frame, and successive arguments are x and y to form the axis. The measuring factor is assigned to the color. The y-axis value should be numeric in increasing or decreasing order to visualize the funnel shape.

```
df = pd.read_csv("population_by_country_2020.csv")
sorted_density = pd.DataFrame().assign(Density=df['Density (P/
sq.Km)'].sort_values(),Country=df['Country'])
Density = px.funnel(sorted_density, x ='Density' , y='Country',
color='Density')

app.layout = html.Div(style = {'width' :1200}, children =
[html.H1('World Density(Population/Sq.Km) Dashboard'),
                    dcc.Graph(figure = Density)
                    ])
```

The example code block depicts the population density increase among the countries in the world. The second statement in the code sorts the density values from the original dataset and the corresponding country to form a sorted_density data frame. Figure 5-18 shows the density for all the countries listed in the dataset; hence, it is more packed. However, Figure 5-19 is limited to 10 countries that are most populated per square kilometer by selecting the last 10 entries. The data in the legend can be enabled or disabled to visualize the selected values for in-depth analysis.

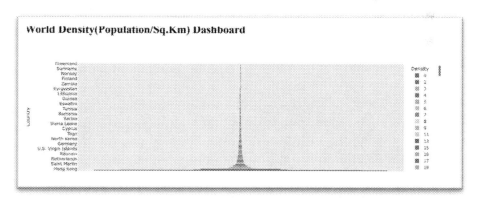

Figure 5-18. *The population density of world countries in increasing order*

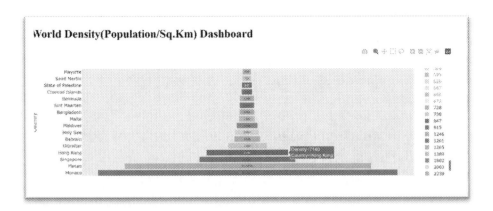

Figure 5-19. *The top 10 countries in population density in increasing order*

Summary

Data visualization plays a crucial role in improving data analysis in businesses. Selecting a suitable type of data visualization is tricky and requires knowledge of all the possible ways to handle the data. Data handling, including its visualization and manipulation, is an art that can make the decision-making process faster and hence improve the business.

CHAPTER 6

Digital Twins for Industry 4.0

A *digital twin* is a computer-generated representation of a physical object, equipment, or service. It can be an automated replica of a real-world object, such as a wind farm, a jet engine, or a larger entity such as an entire city or structure. The digital twin technology can be used to duplicate processes to collect data to forecast future performance. In this chapter, we will cover two concepts of smart industry: smart manufacturing and digital twins. Also, we discuss in detail an application developed for a digital twin based on a windmill.

Smart Industry

Smart manufacturing (SM) is an Internet-connected machine-based method for monitoring manufacturing processes. SM's objective is to automate operations and uncover data-driven possibilities to improve manufacturing performance. SM is an industrial Internet of Things (IIoT) application. Sensors are included in manufacturing machines to collect operational status and performance data throughout deployment. Previously, this information was used only to identify the root cause following a device failure and was saved in a local database for each device.

By evaluating data streaming from the equipment in an entire facility or numerous factories, manufacturing engineers and data analysts can search for indications that certain components are out of order or faulty, thus avoiding equipment downtime. For instance, the SM system can automatically order additional raw materials that are in stock, assign other equipment to production orders as needed to complete the order, and prepare the distribution network once the order has been fulfilled.

Digital twins are the capacity to generate a virtual representation of the physical components and dynamics of an Internet of Things (IoT) device's operation. It is more than just a blueprint or a plan. It is not merely an image. It is not simply "virtual reality" glasses. It is a virtual representation of the elements and dynamics that govern the response of an IoT device throughout its life cycle. There are numerous use cases, including jet engines, structures, manufacturing floor processes, etc.

Digital twins are essentially computer simulations that use data from the actual world to forecast the success of a product or process. These applications can use the IoT, AI, and software analytics to enhance performance. These virtual models are now a vital part of the most recent innovation-driving and performance-improving technologies due to advancements in machine learning and big data. Creating one allows for the improvement of strategic technological trends, the prevention of costly physical object failures, and the utilization of predictive capabilities, services, sophisticated analytics, testing methods, and monitoring.

The digital twin technology begins with applied data science investigating the physics or mathematics and operational data of a system or physical object to develop a mathematical model that simulates the original. Digital twins are created by developers who allow virtual computer models to get feedback from sensors that collect data from the actual version. This enables the digital version to imitate and re-create what is occurring in the original version in real time, providing insights about performance and potential issues.

Digital twins can be as complicated or basic as necessary, with the amount of data dictating how closely the model mimics the actual physical version. The twin can also be used in conjunction with a prototype to provide feedback on the product under development, or as an independent prototype to simulate what occurs to the real version during construction. Figure 6-1 shows real-world applications of a digital twin.

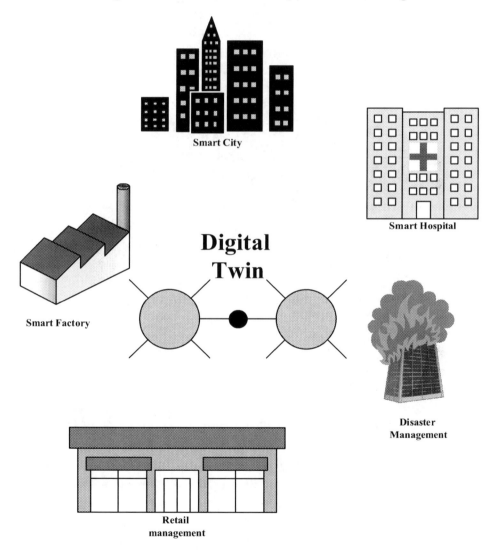

Figure 6-1. *Applications of a digital twin*

Digital Twin Designed for a Windmill

The digital twin design consists of sensors, a communication protocol, a transceiver module, and a digital platform. In this section, we demonstrate a sample digital twin that was created to monitor a local power windmill. Figure 6-2 showcases the digital twin and its components for the digital twin design of a windmill.

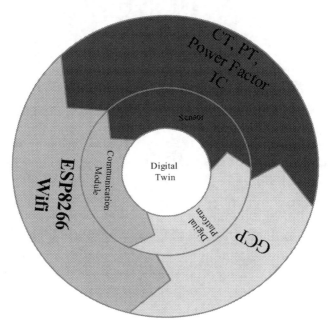

Figure 6-2. *Applications of a digital twin*

A single-phase 1KW windmill is considered here, and its output is connected with a PZEM power meter with CT and PT terminals. The output is connected with the NodeMCU. The firmware to monitor it is as follows:

```
#include <Arduino.h>
#include <ESP8266WiFi.h>
#include "HTTPSRedirect.h"
#include <PZEM004Tv30.h>
```

The Arduino.h library contains the functions and methods for the fundamental usage of Arduino boards and their interfacing. The ESP8266WiFi library supports Wi-Fi access for NodeMCU. The HTTPSRedirect library is mainly included to support communication with servers through an HTTP or HTTPS request. The connection request requires security certificates based on SHA, etc., in order to access the websites. PZEM004Tv30.h is the library for Peacefair energy meter modules with a Modbus interface. The library enables the measurement of voltage, current, power, frequency, etc.

```
PZEM004Tv30 pzem1(D5, D6, 0x01);
// Enter network credentials:
const char* ssid     = "IoT";
const char* password = "IoT@1234";
```

The Peacefair energy meter is connected through TX and RX pins using the function call pzem1(..). All the parameters are read through this connectivity with an energy meter module. Next, Wi-Fi access requires an ID and password, which are specified in the variables ssid and password. The Google script deployment ID is assigned to the variable GScriptId, and the command to insert the row into Google Sheets is framed, as shown in the following snippet:

```
// Enter Google Script Deployment ID:
const char *GScriptId = "**********************************";
String payload_base =  "{\"command\": \"insert_row\", \"sheet_
name\": \"Sheet1\", \"values\": ";
String payload = "";
```

The server connection is established, and the script deployment parameters are initialized to their corresponding values. Port 443 is used for secure communication using HTTPS with the server. A secure

fingerprint to access the server and the script ID for execution are also
initialized in the following code segment:

```
// Google Sheets setup (do not edit)
const char* host = "script.google.com";
const int httpsPort = 443;
const char* fingerprint = "*****";
String url = String("/macros/s/") + GScriptId + "/exec";
HTTPSRedirect* client = nullptr;
```

Pins are allocated for input and output and to read the pulse. Pin 4 is to
enable the slave device.

```
int vs =D0;
int Enable_pin = 4;
int Analog_pin = A0;
int vibration =0 ;
```

The following code establishes a Wi-Fi connection and successively
creates a new secured connection with the server, which has Google Sheets
to update.

```
void setup() {
  Serial.begin(4800);
  pinMode(Enable_pin, OUTPUT);
  pinMode(Analog_pin,INPUT);
  delay(10);
  digitalWrite(Enable_pin, HIGH);
  Serial.println('\n');

  // Connect to WiFi
  WiFi.begin(ssid, password);
  Serial.print("Connecting to ");
  Serial.print(ssid); Serial.println(" ...");
```

```
while (WiFi.status() != WL_CONNECTED) {
  delay(1000);
  //Serial.print(".");
}
Serial.println('\n');
Serial.println("Connection established!");
Serial.print("IP address:\t");
Serial.println(WiFi.localIP());

// Use HTTPSRedirect class to create a new TLS connection
client = new HTTPSRedirect(httpsPort);
client->setInsecure();
client->setPrintResponseBody(true);
client->setContentTypeHeader("application/json");

Serial.print("Connecting to ");
Serial.println(host);
```

The following code segment tries to establish a connection with the server five times. Messages will be displayed accordingly based on the status of the connection.

```
// Try to connect for a maximum of 5 times
  bool flag = false;
  for (int i=0; i<5; i++){
    int retval = client->connect(host, httpsPort);
    if (retval == 1){
        flag = true;
        Serial.println("Connected");
        break;
    }
else
      Serial.println("Connection failed. Retrying...");
  }
```

```
  if (!flag){
    Serial.print("Could not connect to server: ");
    Serial.println(host);
    return;
  }
  delete client;    // delete HTTPSRedirect object
  client = nullptr; // delete HTTPSRedirect object
}

void publish() {

long vibration =pulseIn (vs, HIGH);
    Serial.println(vibration);            //Serial Write ADC_
                                          Value to RS-485 Bus

    float voltagek = pzem1.voltage();
    float currentk = pzem1.current();
    float powerk = pzem1.power();
    float frequencyk = pzem1.frequency();
    float pf = pzem1.pf();
  static bool flag = false;
```

The vibration and other parameters such as voltage current, power, and frequency are read from the energy meter module. The values read from the module are temporarily stored in the variables.

```
  if (!flag){
    client = new HTTPSRedirect(httpsPort);
    client->setInsecure();
    flag = true;
    client->setPrintResponseBody(true);
    client->setContentTypeHeader("application/json");
  }
```

```
if (client != nullptr){
  if (!client->connected()){
    client->connect(host, httpsPort);
  }
}
else{
  Serial.println("Error creating client object!");
}
```

The client connection with the server is established with the previous code. The flag Boolean variable is used to check inside the publish function each time the data is transmitted.

```
// Create json object string to send to Google Sheets
payload = payload_base + "\"" + vibration + "," + voltagek +
"," + currentk + ","+  powerk + "," + frequencyk + "," +
pf +  "\"}";

// Publish data to Google Sheets
Serial.println("Publishing data...");
Serial.println(payload);
if(client->POST(url, host, payload)){
  // do stuff here if publish was successful
}
else{
  // do stuff here if publish was not successful
  Serial.println("Error while connecting");
}
 Serial.println();
 delay(2000);
}
```

The values read in the variables are combined into a JSON object in order to update Google Sheets. The post method is called to transmit the data to the server.

```
void loop() {
  publish();
  delay(100);
}
```

The complete process is repeated periodically to update Google Sheets. A delay of 100 milliseconds is specified between the two successive reads from the energy meter nodule. The corresponding gauges are redrawn based on the current update in Google Sheets in the following code segments.

```
<html>
  <head>
    <h1 id="sensor"><center><bold>NIWE</bold></center></h1>
    <script type="text/javascript" src="https://www.gstatic.com/
    charts/loader.js"></script>
    <script type="text/javascript">

    const sheetID = '1nVWN2HtJ7RcgOprXTMScjmI8NbwOY7DDz
    QIqQQMgkyY';
    const base = 'https://docs.google.com/spreadsheets/
    d/${sheetID}/edit#gid=0';
    const sheetName = 'Sheet1';

    const url =
'https://script.google.com/macros/s/AKfycbx85g1lXOkFDe45_6do2r4
NJfuxZiDvHuwn7j3mnpIYs8aS5z8xKiSMpYfKA-DXtXVK/exec?';

    var sensordata="";
    setInterval(fetchdata, 3000);
    function fetchdata(){
```

```
    const Http = new XMLHttpRequest();
//const url='https://jsonplaceholder.typicode.com/posts';
Http.open("GET", url);
Http.send();
```

The HTML file is designed to receive the data from Google Sheets and display the data in the gauge format. The script fetches data periodically from the sheet by establishing proper connectivity with the sheet using JavaScript and HTML tags. Google Sheets is passed, and the sheet name is specified to retrieve the data from the sheet. The script to read the data and its URL is specified.

```
Http.onreadystatechange = function(){
  if(this.readyState==4 && this.status==200)
{
let sensordata = Http.responseText;
//alert(sensordata);

google.charts.load('current', {
  packages: ['gauge']
}).then(function() {
  var gauge;
  var gaugedata;
  var gaugeOptions = {
    min: 0,
    max: 1000,
    minorTicks: 5,
    animation: {
      duration: 400,
      startup: true,
      easing: 'inAndOut',
    },
};
```

The onreadystatechange property of the http object is checked, which generally defines a function to be called when the readyState property changes. The readyState property indicates the status of the XMLHttpRequest.

- 0: Request not initialized

- 1: Server connection established

- 2: Request received

- 3: Processing request

- 4: Request finished and response is ready

The status property indicates the status of the object.

- Viz 200: "OK"

- 403: "Forbidden"

- 404: "Page not found"

Once the sensor data is received, the Google chart is loaded, and the gauge package is specified. The various options for the gauge to be displayed are set, such as min, max, minor ticks, and animation if required when the values of the sheets are received.

```
let datas = sensordata.split(",");
 var gauge_text1 = datas[0];
 var gauge_text2 = datas[1];
 var gauge_text3 = datas[2];
 var gauge_text4 = datas[3];
 var gauge_text5 = datas[4];
 var gauge_text6 = datas[5];

 gaugeData = new google.visualization.DataTable();
 gaugeData.addColumn('number', 'Vibration');
 gaugeData.addColumn('number', 'Voltage');
```

```
gaugeData.addColumn('number', 'Current');
gaugeData.addColumn('number', 'Power');
gaugeData.addColumn('number', 'Frequency');
gaugeData.addColumn('number', 'PowerFactor');
gaugeData.addRows(1);
gaugeData.setCell(0, 0, gauge_text1, gauge_text1);
gaugeData.setCell(0, 1, gauge_text2, gauge_text2);
gaugeData.setCell(0, 2, gauge_text3, gauge_text3);
gaugeData.setCell(0, 3, gauge_text4, gauge_text4);
gaugeData.setCell(0, 4, gauge_text5, gauge_text5);
gaugeData.setCell(0, 5, gauge_text6, gauge_text6);
```

The received data needs to be split to set the six gauges with their intended values. The first part splits the data into six pieces of text. Six columns are created in the data table for the visualization of gauges. The new row is created in that table. The six data pieces are added in that row under each column, and the gauges are redrawn with the just-updated data.

```
for (var i = 0; i < gaugeData.getNumberOfColumns(); i++) {
  drawGauge(i);
}

var gaugeView;
function drawGauge(index) {
  gaugeView = new google.visualization.DataView(gaugeData);
  gaugeView.setColumns([index]);
  gauge = new google.visualization.Gauge(document.
  getElementById('gauge_div_' + index));
  if (index == 0) {
    gaugeOptions.max = 100;
  }
```

```
    if (index == 1) {
      gaugeOptions.max = 300;
    }
    if (index == 2) {
      gaugeOptions.max = 10;
    }
    if (index == 3) {
      gaugeOptions.min = -1;
      gaugeOptions.max = 1;
    }
    if (index == 4) {
      gaugeOptions.min = 49;
      gaugeOptions.max = 51;
    }
    if (index == 5) {
      gaugeOptions.min = -1;
      gaugeOptions.max = 1;
    }
    gauge.draw(gaugeView, gaugeOptions);
  }
});
}
}
}
</script>
```

The above code block defines how the six gauges are drawn in the HTML page. The function drawGauge is defined to display six gauges with its minimum and maximum values. The gauges range is fixed based on its parameter for which the gauge is meant. The gauge is identified with the indices 0, 1, 2, 3, 4, and 5.

```
<style>
  h1 {
background-color : rgb(144, 144, 212);
color: black;
}
.wrapper {
  white-space: normal;
}
.gauge {
  display: inline-block;
  height: 2050px;
  width: 400px;
}
html,body
 {
    padding:0;
    margin:0;
    align: center;
    height:100%;
    min-height:100%;
  }
.part1 {background-color:rgb(147, 147, 158); width:30%;
height:45%; float:left}
.part2 {background-color:rgb(147, 147, 158); width:30%;
height:45%; float:left}
.part3 {background-color:rgb(147, 147, 158); width:38.5%;
height:45%; float:left}
.part4 {background-color:rgb(147, 147, 158); width:30%;
height:45%; float:left}
.part5 {background-color:rgb(147, 147, 158); width:30%;
height:45%; float:left}
```

```
.part6 {background-color:rgb(147, 147, 158); width:38.5%;
height:45%; float:left}
</style>
</head>
```

The display style of each component in HTML is defined inside the style tag. The color of the background of the heading and six parts in the body of the HTML are also defined. The wrapper block is to center the content to be displayed in the web page. The gauge part is to define the window size using height and width attributes.

```
    <body>
  <script src="https://www.gstatic.com/charts/loader.
js"></script>
<div class="wrapper">
  <div class="part1" id="gauge_div_0"></div>
  <div class="part2" id="gauge_div_1"></div>
  <div class="part3" id="gauge_div_2"></div>
  <div class="part4" id="gauge_div_3"></div>
  <div class="part5" id="gauge_div_4"></div>
  <div class="part6" id="gauge_div_5"></div>
</div>
  </body>
</html>
```

The loader needs to be loaded with the first line of script. The div tag is used as a container of various HTML components whose styles are defined already in the previous script. Based on the previous code blocks, the data filled by NodeMCU in Google Sheets is showcased in Figure 6-3, and the corresponding changes in the gauges are depicted in Figure 6-4. You can see the simple gauge-type GUI designed for monitoring the windmill operation and vibrations.

	DATE	TIME	VIBRATION	VOLTAGE	CURRENT	POWER	FREQUENCY	POWER_FACTOR
1	**DATE**	**TIME**	**VIBRATION**	**VOLTAGE**	**CURRENT**	**POWER**	**FREQUENCY**	**POWER_FACTO**
2	2022/11/02	12:02:58 PM	0	229	8	1778	50	1
3	2022/11/02	12:02:51 PM	0	230	8	1778	50	1
4	2022/11/02	12:02:42 PM	0	228	8	1775	50	1
5	2022/11/02	12:02:35 PM	0	232	8	1788	50	1
6	2022/11/02	12:02:26 PM	0	232	8	1787	50	1
7	2022/11/02	12:02:19 PM	0	232	8	1786	50	1
8	2022/11/02	12:02:12 PM	0	232	8	1786	50	1
9	2022/11/02	12:02:05 PM	0	232	8	1784	50	1
10	2022/11/02	12:01:57 PM	0	232	8	1779	50	1
11	2022/11/02	12:01:50 PM	0	232	8	1775	50	1
12	2022/11/02	12:01:43 PM	0	232	8	1784	50	1
13	2022/11/02	12:01:35 PM	0	232	8	1808	50	1
14	2022/11/02	12:01:28 PM	0	232	8	1879	50	1
15	2022/11/02	12:00:16 PM	0	234	8	1788	50	1
16	2022/11/02	12:00:09 PM	0	233	8	1785	50	1
17	2022/11/02	12:00:02 PM	0	233	8	1782	50	1
18	2022/11/02	11:59:54 AM	0	233	8	1778	50	1
19	2022/11/02	11:59:46 AM	0	233	8	1767	50	1
20	2022/11/02	11:59:39 AM	0	233	8	1762	50	1
21	2022/11/02	11:59:31 AM	0	233	8	1769	50	1

Figure 6-3. *Google Sheets platform*

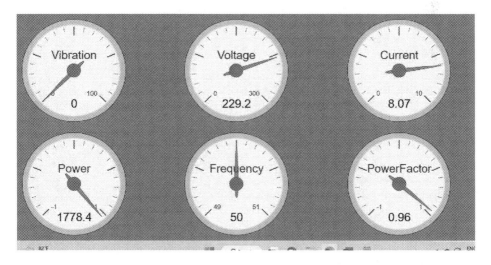

Figure 6-4. *Dashboard showcasing a digital twin of a windmill*

195

Companies can create value, develop new revenue streams, and find strategic solutions with the aid of digital twins. Organizations can set out on a journey to create digital twins with less capital investment and time value than ever before thanks to new technology capabilities. Digital twins have an essentially limitless future as more and more cognitive power is employed. Because digital twins are always picking up new skills and abilities, it is possible to keep producing the insights required to improve processes and create better goods in the future.

Summary

The prediction of future performance of any physical machine can be performed through a virtual clone, called a digital twin. The predictions in turn prevent future failures and provide insights into how to handle certain scenarios in a well-planned way. In this chapter, we looked at applying digital twin technology in smart industries. Also, we demonstrated a digital twin design and a windmill as a physical digital fusion. In the next chapter, you will look at industrial IoT in supply chain management.

CHAPTER 7

Supply Chain Monitoring

In this chapter, we will explore supply chain management including supply chain strategies, industry operations, supply chain performance measures, and supply chain technologies. First, let's establish just what a supply chain is.

What Is a Supply Chain?

A *supply chain* is the process of manufacturing a product from the raw materials through delivering the product to the end customer. The supply chain definition in the real world is not that simple, though. A network of people and organizations is involved in this chain. The chain starts at the raw material producer and ends at the customer who buys the product. In between the start and end of the link, there are many components such as transporting the various raw materials from their place of origin to one or more warehouses and to the product manufacturing location based on the requirements. After the production of the product, the product is distributed to the various distribution centers or vendors based on demand and in turn to the retailers and storerooms of online sellers. The success of any business is based on smart planning management of the supply chain.

© G.R. Kanagachidambaresan, Bharathi N. 2023
G.R. Kanagachidambaresan and N. Bharathi, *Sensors and Protocols for Industry 4.0*,
Maker Innovations Series, https://doi.org/10.1007/978-1-4842-9007-1_7

Supply chain management is the management of the stream from raw materials to end product. It's necessary to plan and organize the activities and processes involved in the supply chain to maximize the production and satisfy the customer demands at the same time. Supply chain management is one of the key factors to keep a competitive position in the marketplace. Experts in the supply chain suggest many different strategies for supply chain management.

Supply Chain Strategies

There are different supply chain strategies to handle the processes involved in transforming raw materials to a complete product. The main objective of any strategy is to optimize the overall value across the supply chain. There are various stages involved in supply chain management, and the strategy provides the mechanisms to handle every stage. Supply chain strategies help companies to meet the demands of their customers with fewer misperceptions and ensure the functioning of every stage in an optimized manner. A strategy encompasses trade-offs between the efficiency, elasticity, and coordination and the predominant goal of the business. The following are the key factors that influence the organization's strategy:

- Overall operational procedure of the industry

- Adapting standards

- Internal decision-making policies

- Company value across the globe or geographical area

- Primary objective and goals of the business

The supply chain strategies are categorized into two major divisions: business strategy and organizational strategy.

Business Strategy

A *business strategy* focuses on minimum cost, differentiation, and marketing focus. Minimum cost means the product should have the lowest price compared to competitors that are selling an equivalent product. The differentiation is the model, the features of product, or the service options that are different from the competitor. The marketing focus is defined as the product or service being developed for a specific audience such as kids or a broad audience. Some manufacturers use a hybrid of the previous three business strategies.

Organizational Strategy

The business strategy is the primary goal for some companies, while others follow hybrid strategies, which may include organizational and supply chain strategies that are in line with the business strategies. For example, product differentiation and specific audience can be combined without any mutual exclusiveness, whereas low cost and high quality are not fit to combine. The *organizational strategy* defines how to satisfy customers, manage organizations, improve the capabilities within the business, etc.

The business, organizational, and supply chain strategies play key roles when multiple firms are collectively trying to achieve a common goal. Hence, the strategies need to be aligned with each other to achieve short-term as well as long-term business goals. Along with these strategies, collaboration, time, and location are the key elements that contribute to the strength of supply chain management.

The following strategies have been in practice since 2021 to meet demand surges and logistics difficulties and/or external unexpected situations:

- **Reserve space across the supply chain stages**: The main supply chain stages are upstream and downstream. Upstream is from the various suppliers of raw materials and the manufacturer. Downstream is between the manufacturer and the delivery centers, retailers, and finally end customers. The reserved space is divided into two categories; one is storage scale, and the other one is in time scale. The reserved storage space is required to meet the unexpected demand surge, which can be solved by warehouses and inventory for finished goods and raw materials. The reserved time space is necessary to handle the unexpected delay in logistics and movement of goods.

- **Always have a plan B to deal with unexpected scenarios**: Many industrial experts suggest having alternative plans so you can overcome unexpected situations. The supply chain is a complex network that can be made simpler through proper planning and being able to handle unexpected situations. Clearance sales, discount sales, and limited editions are some examples to overcome losses.

- **Expanding the upstream and downstream**: The upstream is procuring raw materials from the suppliers. The downstream is delivering end products to distribution centers. In both upstream and downstream, the managers or executives should not rely on a single source or limited sources, which may lead to riskier situations to meet demand surge, natural disasters, and similar situations. The number of suppliers and distribution centers needs to be increased to deal with sparse raw materials and stagnation in distributing the finished goods.

- **Invest in supply chain management for achieving long-term success**: It is necessary to spend some money to develop the business. The amount spent for supply chain management is an investment. It's an investment into growing the business, and it is mandatory nowadays in this ever-changing global market. The supply chain management and strategies can improve the business steadily even in the presence of downturns in profit. The overall long-term goal needs to be scheduled on the timeline, and parts of it will be achieved periodically over time.

- **Regulate the process and standardize the protocol involved**: Producing a product from the supplied raw materials, distributing the product to the retailers through distribution centers, and finally selling it to the end users are all based on certain procedures and protocols. The protocols and procedures need to be followed always and standardized based on the internal policies and standards bodies. The standards are always helpful in expanding the business across the world to ensure compatibility between individual components.

The ability to easily adapt to the changing frequency of the global market and proactively respond to the demands are the challenges involved in supply chain strategies. Establishing a supply chain strategy with the current global market is crucial, and at the same time it is mandatory for optimizing the value of the business. In the initial stages, the global leaders focus on the efficiency of the supply chain, which reduces the waste and delivers the product more quickly. After COVID-19, the strategy shifted toward resilience to meet the long-term success in the global market even in unexpected circumstances. The benefits of a resilience strategy are a shorter product life cycle, improved productivity, and less risk.

Industry Operations with Supply Chain

Generally, the industry supply chain operations consist of procuring raw materials, storing them in the warehouse, transporting them to the production unit, producing products, transporting products to delivery centers or warehouses, and finally moving them to retail shops or end customers who ordered them online. Figure 7-1 shows the complete process.

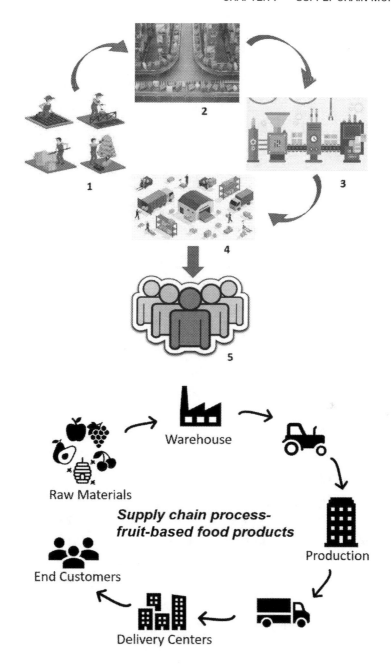

Figure 7-1. *General process of industry operations with a supply chain*

The process is viewed as simple, but monitoring and optimizing the whole process are complex tasks and subject to change. The process can be analyzed with the help of a Python program using a linear programming model, and the status is displayed through a dashboard.

```
import pandas as pd
import NumPy as np

from pulp import *

from dash import Dash, dcc, html
import plotly.express as px
```

The supply chain information can be easily collected and stored in a table format. The Panda library is imported in order to work with dataframe objects, which reads the table as input from various file formats such as text, CSV, XLSX, SQL database, etc. The dataframe object is flexible and manipulated easily as it is indexed. The various methods are available to handle data in the dataframe for missing data, automatic labeling, alignment, converting to numerical values, subsetting the larger datasets, etc.

The NumPy library is imported to handle arrays that hold the intermediate results and that can be analyzed. PuLP is a Python package that solves linear programming (LP) optimization problems. The various industries such as manufacturing, pharmaceuticals, etc., are using LP-based models to optimize their supply chain stream. The dash, dcc, html, and Plotly.express components are included to develop a dashboard for displaying the status information. Tables 7-1 to 7-5 are required for generating the models are read as input either in CSV or XLSX format, and the corresponding index needs to be set for further processing. The capacity of the warehouse is initialized at 10000.

```
inflow= pd.read_excel('inflow.xlsx')
inflow= inflow.set_index('WHS')
Requirement= pd.read_excel('Requirement.xlsx')
Requirement= Requirement.set_index('shop')
outflow= pd.read_excel('outflow.xlsx')
outflow= outflow.set_index('WHS')
PU_costs= pd.read_excel('PU_cost.xlsx')
PU_costs= PU_costs.set_index('PU')
WH_costs= pd.read_excel('WH_costs.xlsx')
WH_costs= WH_costs.set_index('WHS')
WH_costs['Capacity']=10000
```

Table 7-1. *inflow.xlsx (From Warehouse to Production Unit)*

WHS	PU 1	PU 2	PU 3
WH_1	22	71	79
WH_2	64	27	26
WH_3	72	36	56
WH_4	50	75	56
WH_5	32	33	21

Table 7-2. *Requirement of Each Retail Shop*

shop	Requirement
Shop 1	881
shop 2	806
Shop 3	704
Shop 4	767
Shop 5	575
Shop 6	741
Shop 7	593
Shop 8	708
Shop 9	800

Table 7-3. *outflow.xlsx (From Delivery Center to Shop)*

WHS	Shop 1	shop 2	Shop 3	Shop 4	Shop 5	Shop 6	Shop7	Shop 8	Shop 9
WH_1	98	67	103	117	94	116	75	104	103
WH_2	109	85	114	50	64	53	46	62	50
WH_3	57	116	57	119	53	63	106	74	75
WH_4	113	57	92	80	56	77	55	80	92
WH_5	84	73	91	77	98	85	46	58	112

Table 7-4. *Production Unit Operation Cost*

PU	Var	Capacity	Fixed Cost
PU 1	18	3000	40000
PU 2	22	5000	60000
PU 3	32	4000	50000

Table 7-5. *Warehouse Operation Cost*

WHS	Variable Cost	Fixed Cost
WH_1	12	20000
WH_2	15	22000
WH_3	18	40000
WH_4	45	50000
WH_5	23	60000

The indices are assigned to separate objects to manipulate each record in the tables.

```
PU= PU_costs.index
WHs= WH_costs.index
shops= Requirement.index

inflow_keys= [(w,p)for w in WHs for p in PU ]
outflow_keys= [(w,s)for w in WHs for s in shops]

inflow_var= LpVariable.dicts('inflow',inflow_keys,0,None,'Integer')
outflow_var= LpVariable.dicts('outflow',outflow_keys,0,None,
'Integer')
open_WH= LpVariable.dicts('open_WH', WHs,cat='Binary')
open_PU=LpVariable.dicts('open_p',PU,cat='Binary')
```

The inflow constitutes the warehouses for the production unit, and not all are operating in order to accomplish a requirement. Similarly, the outflow constitutes the production units to warehouses; also not all are operating. The inflow and outflow keys are identified based on the operating cost and to minimize the cost. The variables open_WH and open_PU are the operating warehouses and production units for the requirement.

inflow_cost= lpSum(inflow_var[(w,p)] inflow.loc[w,p] for p in PU for w in WHs)*
outflow_cost= lpSum(outflow_var[(w,s)] outflow.loc[w,s] for w in WHs for s in shops)*
production_cost= lpSum(inflow_var[(w,p)] PU_costs.loc[p,'Var'] for p in PU for w in WHs)*
*opening_PU_cost= lpSum(open_PU[(p)]*PU_costs.loc[p, 'fixed cost'] for p in PU)*
opening_WH_cost= lpSum(open_WH[(w)] WH_costs.loc[w, 'Fixed Cost'] for w in WHs)*
*WH_operaing_cost=lpSum(inflow_var[(w,p)]*WH_costs.loc[w,'Variable Cost'] for w in WHs for p in PU)*

Various costs in involved in production

> **Inflow costs**: These are the costs incurred in moving raw materials from the warehouse to the production unit.

> **Outflow costs**: These are the costs incurred in moving products from the production unit to delivery centers.

> **Production cost**: This is the cost incurred in the production of the product (operating costs).

> **Opening_PU_cost**: This is the cost incurred in utilizing the production unit (only a fixed cost).

Opening_WH_cost: This is the cost incurred in utilizing the warehouse (only a fixed cost).

WH_operating_cost: This is the cost incurred in operating the warehouse.

The production optimization is solved by calling linear programming function which optimizes the production with minimized utilization of warehouses.

```
scm_model= LpProblem('Extended1',LpMinimize)

scm_model += (inflow_cost +outflow_cost +production_cost+
opening_PU_cost+ opening_WH_cost+WH_operaing_cost)

for s in shops :
    scm_model += lpSum(outflow_var[(w,s)]for w in WHs)>=
    Requirement.loc[s,'Requirement']
```

The model is not restricted to use a particular number of warehouses. Based on minimizing the optimization, the required warehouses are involved in storage.

```
for p in PU:
    scm_model += lpSum(inflow_var[(w,p)]for w in WHs)
    <= lpSum(PU_costs.loc[p,'capacity']*open_PU[(p)])

for w in WHs:
    scm_model += lpSum(inflow_var[(w,p)] for p in PU)
    <= lpSum(WH_costs.loc[w,'Capacity']*open_WH[(w)])
```

The capacity constraints are defined as the total inflow from the warehouses to a production unit and should not exceed the capacity of that opened production unit. Also, the total production from the units to a warehouse should not exceed the capacity of that opened warehouse.

```
for w in WHs:
    scm_model += lpSum(inflow_var[(w,p)] for p in PU)== lpSum
    (outflow_var[(w,s)] for s in shops)
scm_model += lpSum(open_WH[(w)] for w in WHs)>=1
scm_model += lpSum(open_WH[(w)] for w in WHs)<=5

scm_model += lpSum(open_PU[(p)] for p in PU) >=1
scm_model += lpSum(open_PU[(p)] for p in PU) <=3
```

The products that are generated in the production unit must be equal
to the raw materials entered into the production unit. It is not mandatory
that all the warehouses and production units need to be open for the
required demand. Also, it is not fixed that only specific warehouses and
production units need to be operated.

```
dist_matrix={ (w,s):1 if outflow.loc[w,s] <= 80 else 0 for w
in WHs for s in shops}
total_Requirement= sum(Requirement['Requirement'])
scm_model +=  lpSum(outflow_var[(w,s)]* dist_matrix[(w,s)] for
w in WHs for s in shops)/total_Requirement >= 0.95

scm_model.solve()
```

The distance between the delivery centers and shops is restricted to 80
units. The overall efficiency expected is specified as 95 percent, and hence
the model performance is configured to optimize for 0.95.

```
for v in scm_model.variables():
    print(v.name, "=", v.varValue)

current_service_level= lpSum(outflow_var[(w,s)].varValue* dist_
matrix[(w,s)] for w in WHs for s in shops)/total_Requirement

scm_model.writeLP('extended_model.txt')

binding= [{'constraint': name, 'slack': c.slack} for name,c in
scm_model.constraints.items()]
```

The previous code block analyzes the list of variables in the model and the current service level, which is expected to be greater than 95 percent. The entire model along with the constraints is recorded in a text file for further optimizing possibilities. The binding of constraints and their slack values is observed. The final cost will be changed if any slack value is changed; it can be analyzed and studied by changing the slack values if required.

```python
WH_count = []
PU_1variable = []
PU_2variable = []
PU_3variable = []
count = 1
for opWH in open_WH:
    WH_count.append(count)
    count +=1
for WH in WHs:
    PU_1variable.append(inflow_var[WH,PU[0]].varValue)
    PU_2variable.append(inflow_var[WH,PU[1]].varValue)
    PU_3variable.append(inflow_var[WH,PU[2]].varValue)
data1 = {
  "index":WH_count,
  "WHs":WHs,
  "PU1": PU_1variable,
  "PU2": PU_2variable,
  "PU3": PU_3variable
}
df = pd.read_excel('outflow1.xlsx')

app = Dash(title = 'Supply Chain Network model- Dashboard
Illustration')
df1 = pd.DataFrame(data1)
```

```
bifchart1 = px.bar(inflow, x="WH_id", y="PU 1", color =
"WH_id", title = 'Ware houses distance to PU1')
bifchart2 = px.bar(inflow, x="WH_id", y="PU 2", color =
"WH_id", title = 'Ware houses distance to PU2')
bifchart3 = px.bar(inflow, x="WH_id", y="PU 3", color =
"WH_id", title = 'Ware houses distance to PU3')
sbchart = px.sunburst(df,path=['WHS','shop'],values='Distance' )
chart = px.bar(df, x="WHS", y= "Distance", color= "shop",
barmode="group")
chart1 = px.pie(df1, values = 'PU1',names = 'WHs',
title = 'production in unit 1')
chart2 = px.pie(df1, values = 'PU2',names = 'WHs',
title = 'production in unit 2')
chart3 = px.pie(df1, values = 'PU3',names = 'WHs',
title = 'production in unit 3')
```

The NumPy arrays and dataframes are initialized, and the values are stored to use them for dashboards. The outflow information, i.e., the movement of product from delivery centers to shops, is read for the purpose of displaying it in the dashboard. The dashboard is initiated using the dataframe created. Various charts such as bar charts, sunburst charts, and pie charts are generated using the Plotly Express object and functions.

```
app.layout = html.Div(children=[
        html.H1(children='SCM network model Dashboard'),
        html.Div([
            html.Div([
                dcc.Graph(id='bar-graph1',figure=bifchart1),
                dcc.Graph( id='first-graph', figure=chart1),
                ], style={'width': '33%', 'display':
                'inline-block'},
                className = 'sixcolumns'),
```

```python
        html.Div([
            dcc.Graph(id='bar-graph2',figure=bifchart2),
            dcc.Graph( id='second-graph', figure=chart2),
            ], style={'width': '33%', 'display':
            'inline-block'},
            className = 'sixcolumns'),
        html.Div([
            dcc.Graph(id='bar-graph3',figure=bifchart3),
            dcc.Graph( id='third-graph', figure=chart3),
            ], style={'width': '33%', 'display':
            'inline-block'},
            className = 'sixcolumns'),
        ], className = 'row'),
    html.Div([
        html.Div([
            dcc.Graph(id='out-graph',figure=chart),
        ], style={'width': '50%', 'display':
        'inline-block'},
        className = 'sixcolumns'),
        html.Div([
            dcc.Graph(id='sb-graph1',figure=sbchart),
        ], style={'width': '50%', 'display':
        'inline-block'},
        className = 'sixcolumns'),
        ],className = 'row'),
    ], className = 'parent')


if __name__ == '__main__':
    app.run_server(debug=True, use_reloader=False)
```

The layout is divided into three regions vertically. The first region displays the distances between the warehouses and the production units using bar charts. The second region is displaying the amount of production done in production units; it is depicting that only 2 units are involved in production. The third region is showing distances between the delivery centers and shops in two different charts, grouped bar charts and sunburst charts; see Figure 7-2, Figure 7-3, and Figure 7-4.

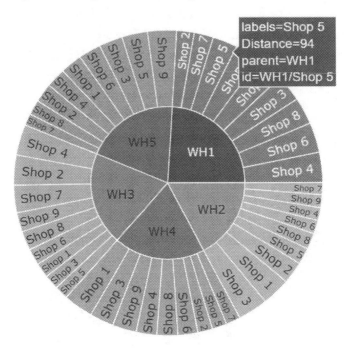

Figure 7-2. *Distance between warehouse and shop (sunburst chart)*

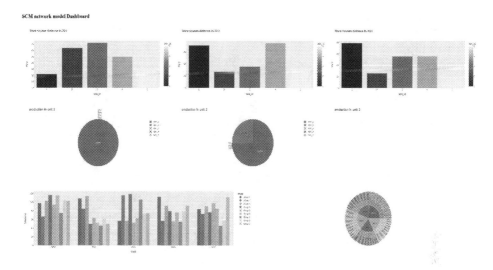

Figure 7-3. *The sample dashboard to display the status of the supply chain stream*

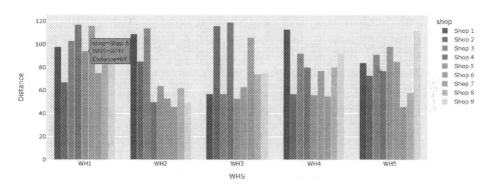

Figure 7-4. *Distance between warehouses and shops (group bar chart)*

Supply Chain Performance Measures

The performance measures are the key factor to determine how well the method or model is working. Supply chain management is not an exception, and it has the following performance measures that can determine the benefits of practices and models in the supply chain:

- **Cash-to-cash time**: This metric defines the period between the time instant at which a business pays for its suppliers and the time at which it receives the cash from its end customers. This time is crucial and decides the success of the business because within this time only the complete production is happening. The amount of investment spent will be converted to cash flow during this time. This measure is based on the three ratios, namely, days of inventory (DOI), days of payables (DOP), and days of receivables (DOR).

- **Supply chain cycle time**: This metric depicts the time it takes to complete an order when the inventory stock is depleted. This metric serves the purpose of understanding the overall efficiency of supply chain management. This consists of the time taken to place an order and receive supplies in inventory and the time taken to produce and deliver the order. The second measure is also called the *order fulfilment cycle time*.

- **Customer order cycle time**: This time metric is for measuring the responsiveness of the supply chain, i.e., how intuitively the company serves the customer order. It describes the number of days between when the company receives the order from the customer and when the product is delivered to the customer. The customer order cycle time is measured as the date and time the purchase order is placed subtracted from the actual delivery date and time. It is the time span between placing the order and receiving the product from the customer perspective.

- **Perfect order index**: The perfect order index is the measure that defines the faultless delivery of the product during the entire supply chain. Faultless delivery includes the placing of orders correctly, delivered on time with ordered quantities, and received by the customer without any damage. The perfect order index is calculated as ((total orders – order with errors or faults) / total orders)/100.

- **Gross margin returns on investment (GMROI)**: The inventory investments are periodical expenses based on the orders. This metric is used to figure out how well inventory investments are performing. GMROI defines the profit gained on a particular inventory investment. The reason for a GMROI decrease or increase can be devised from this measure. An improvement in GMROI could be because of high-quality raw materials from specific suppliers. The GMROI as a percentage can be calculated using the formula gross profit / ((opening inventory for a specific period – closing inventory during that period)/2) × 100.

- **Total supply chain management cost as percentage of sales**: In general, the supply chain costs are the combination of inventory cost, transportation cost, investment cost, procurement cost, production cost, etc. This is the measure that defines the investment in supply chain management. It also describes how much

percentage of its sales a company can invest in supply
chain management in order to improve the business.
This metric is calculated as (overall supply chain cost/
total sales) × 100.

- **Inventory investment**: Inventory investment is
  the amount spent on a raw material, production in
  progress, product inventory, etc., to achieve the assured
  service targets even in the existence of fluctuating
  demand, forecasting inaccuracy, long lead times, lack
  of transport capacity, etc. It is a percentage of gross or
  net profit calculated for an item or a location based on
  the targets, demand, and lead time.

- **Inventory turnover**: This metric defines the frequency
  of selling the entire inventory over a specific period of
  time. The inventory turnover is measured as costs of
  goods sold in a period divided by average inventory.
  A high value for inventory turnover depicts that the
  business is making a profit. If this value is lower, then it
  indicates the excess inventory and lags in sales.

- **Forecasting accuracy**: This measure explains how
  to expand the business in the future. It predicts
  the demand of the product in the future from the
  feedback of the customers through various sources.
  The forecasting depends on the industry type and
  the ability to envision the demand. It is measured in
  many ways, and a 30-day, 60-day, or 90-day outlook is
  followed widely. The forecasting error determines the
  accuracy by deriving the difference between the actual
  demand and the forecasted demand. Two methods
  of calculating the forecasting error are the mean
  absolute percent error (MAPE) formula and the mean

absolute deviation (MAD) formula. The MAPE formula calculates the APE first as ((actual demand – forecast demand)/ Actual demand) × 100 and computes the mean M as an error percentage over the given time period. The MAD is computed as a deviation in forecast demand from actual demand.

- **Fill rate**: One of the important metrics for defining the efficiency of the company is the fill rate. It depicts the brand reputation and customer fulfilment levels. The fill rate for orders delivered, individual items delivered, order of a day delivered on first effort, etc., can be set as benchmarks. Any inconsistencies in fill rate will uncover the reason for not fulfilling the order and show how to improve it. Fill rate also assesses the performance of supply chain management. It can be derived as ((1-total products – shipped products)/total products) × 100.

- **Back order**: This measure describes the orders that do not reach customers on time because of supply chain delay. It is complementary to the fill rate metric. It is calculated as the ratio of orders not delivered on time to the total orders. The supply chain can maintain the threshold values of back orders; if a value goes higher, a warning circular can be sent to the concerned supply chain team. Frequent back orders with a large time delay signify something is wrong and needs to change in the procedure of handling orders.

- **On-time shipping**: This metric states the time taken to ship a particular item to a customer. It is a good indicator for setting the benchmark shipping time for each product. Improving the shipping time improves the turnaround time and customer fulfilment. The metric is measured as the ratio of placed orders shipped on or before the scheduled delivery date to the total orders placed. The product delivery performance can be tracked easily with this measure. The higher the value of this measure, the greater the efficiency of the supply chain management. It also helps in avoiding customer dissatisfaction, which may lead to losing them.

The supply chain metrics play a key role in enhancing the performance of the supply chain management system, which in turn measures the progress of attaining any industrial goals. Every activity is monitored and serves as input for the supply chain metrics and is consequently used to analyze performance. Analysis should be done on a routine basis, because a metric may forecast better performance but then become worse after several months. Hence, before any performance metric declines, the team involved in contributing to that metric needs to be informed so they can change their behavior to meet the goal. It's also important to communicate the metrics to the team involved quickly to help them understand their part in improving the metric. Various kinds of feedback need to happen regularly such as score boards, meetings, reviews, etc., to improve the overall performance.

Supply Chain Technologies

Emerging technologies are impacting almost all domains, and the supply chain is not an exception. Companies are now digitizing the supply chain. The correct technology adoption by organizations creates a competitive advantage when compared to competitors. Supply chain technologies are contributing to decision-making and asset management. Companies are expanding across the world, products have shorter life spans in the market, and customers are expecting new products every day. Further, improvements can be achieved by following a unified technology profile. The following five technologies are necessary for supply chain digitization and in turn digital supply chain twins.

Internet of Things and the Cloud

The location of the supply chain vehicles, environmental conditions, real-time traffic, etc., can be tracked and monitored with the IoT and the cloud. For example, the freshness of the foods in the supply chain can be monitored periodically, and the delivery can be sped up well before the expiry date. In addition, with this tracking and monitoring, the assets are safeguarded while moving from the manufacturing plant to the retailer, and any loss is prevented.

Edge computing combines the benefit of cloud computing for IoT-based systems and provides an ecosystem for the various components such as devices, sensors, actuators, robots, drones, etc., to work together toward a goal. So, with the supply chain, the edge ecosystem plays a predominant role in tracking and decision-making. However, the IoT is vulnerable in regard to security.

Machine Learning and Analytics

Machine learning comprises complex algorithms that are interesting and can solve many issues across many industries. It enables waste reduction and improves quality analytically. It optimizes the flow of a product in the supply chain without any backup in inventory. It also helps predict future market behavior with data analytics. The following are some of the machine learning use cases followed in the supply chain: predictive analytics, streamlining of production, reduced cost and time of production and overall supply chain, warehouse management, etc. The popular companies that are employing machine learning to improve their supply chain management are Microsoft, Procter & Gamble, Rolls Royce, etc. Conclusively, machine learning makes dealing with the challenges like an instable and ever-changing global market easier and can forecast product demand accurately at a global level.

Blockchain

The supply chain works well with block technology because of the distributed ledger in blockchain. The public ledger is read and written to without any permission and records the day-to-day activity of the supply chain. The private ledger, which requires permission to read or write to, can be used by officials to record major events and decisions. The blockchain generates immutable transactions, which is required for supply chain management. The immutability assures that the record cannot be erased. The trust established using the blockchain can verify the goods delivered or supplied to or from the legitimate destination or source, respectively. The audit trail generated in the blockchain acts as a key factor to use the blockchain technology not only in the supply chain but also in the other business domains in which object tracking exists. A real-world example where blockchain is used in the supply chain is at Bumble Bee Foods, where it tracks the journey of yellow fin tuna from the ocean to the dinner table.

Robots and Automation

In general, robots are designed to support activities that are difficult for humans or that require more human resources. Moving heavy goods is one task where robots can be helpful. Other uses are picking and aligning products in the production flow, packing finished orders, and removing hazardous or medical wastes.

Cobots (collaborative robots) are new-generation robots that combine the features of machine learning, IoT connectivity, and distributed systems. They work along with humans by taking care of the safety of goods and their mobility path. Cobots are resolving the constraints of labor availability, labor rates in distribution centers, and warehouses to lift heavy weights when loading and unloading bays.

Using robots or cobots is a boon to industries because they reduce human errors when doing repetitive tasks. The robots are configured to do a task in the same manner every time the task is performed. Automation can be easily realized in industry with the usage of robots instead of humans.

Digital Supply Chain Twin

A simulation model of a real supply chain process that depicts the flow of goods from raw material to end product is known as a *digital supply chain twin*. Obviously, the digital twin of a supply chain helps in understanding the flow of goods, in finding the potential pitfalls in overall performance, in decision-making, in forecasting, etc. The live data stream is always available for viewing the current performance and predicting the future. The digital supply chain twin is developed with an interconnected network of software, sensors, and tracking devices that are interoperable and equipped with controlling interfaces and alarms. The controlling interfaces are enabled based on the flow of goods, demand, and other requirements. The alarms are activated to predict abnormal scenarios in the supply chain. The twin also helps in testing a new development in supply chain management by adopting it in the existing simulation model without incorporating it in the real flow.

Summary

Supply chain management is mutually dependent on the industrial Internet of Things. The strategies that define the supply chain are business and organizational strategies. They govern the operations in the supply chain at every stage. The stages of the supply chain start from raw material procurement and end at delivering the product to the end user. The success of supply chain management can be analyzed and studied with various performance metrics. The procedure involved in the supply chain should be continuously monitored with the industrial Internet of Things and optimized from time to time to adapt the changes evolving in the industrial and technological world. We learned about the industrial domain that uses the IoT to monitor and control and in decision-making. In the next chapter, we will discuss Node-RED programming, which uses simple drag-and-drop blocks for programming and where the outcomes of real-time systems are monitored and controlled visually.

CHAPTER 8

Introduction to Node-RED and Industrial Dashboard Design

Industry 4.0 applications are realized with cyber physical systems. Cyber physical systems (CPSs) can be designed, developed, and deployed in several ways. The most promising approach that provides real-world connectivity between the cyber and physical worlds is through Node-RED programming. In this chapter, we'll detail why Node-RED is the best and most effective solution for cyber physical systems. The following are the topics we'll cover in the course of this chapter:

- An overview of Node-RED

- The building blocks of Node-RED

- Writing a simple program in Node-RED

© G.R. Kanagachidambaresan, Bharathi N. 2023
G.R. Kanagachidambaresan and N. Bharathi, *Sensors and Protocols for Industry 4.0*,
Maker Innovations Series, https://doi.org/10.1007/978-1-4842-9007-1_8

Why Node-RED?

Node-RED programming can unite the functionality of hardware with web services. The Node-RED libraries provide the low-level coding for interfacing any two devices, and the process can be as simple as connecting two devices visually by dragging and dropping.

Most browsers support Node-RED programming, and hence integrating it into web applications is simpler than any other method. In addition, it executes in a lightweight environment as it is developed on Node.js and can be executed and tested on a local machine using Docker support. The runtime environment provides an event-driven approach in a nonblocking manner, which enables responses to the events in a well-organized way. The flow that is built using Node-RED programming can be easily ported into JSON format and used in any other flow as a subflow. Also, the programming can be ported to various devices such as BeagleBone Black, the Raspberry Pi, etc., and it can be executed in cloud environments such as AWS, IBM-Bluemix, etc. The JavaScript language is used for simple coding to pass parameters and messages as input and to display the output. Node-RED is useful for rapid prototyping and demonstrating the working principles of any industry-based applications. However, it is slow in performance when compared to other servers such as Java servers.

Node-RED is an easy-to-use drag-and-drop programming environment developed by Nick O'Leary and Dave Conway-Jones. It provides an easy way for shopfloor workers and industrialists to learn the IoT platform. Node-RED is graphical user interface (GUI) programming environment to develop real-time systems with visual outcomes on the go. It was declared open-source and released in 2014. Many researchers have started contributing to Node-RED. The design of CPSs through single-board computers (SBCs) is presently carried out through Node-RED for fast and ease deployment. Open-source contributors to this community provide frequent updates based on current marketing demands and processor availability. Hence, updates for Node-RED are released frequently, so programmers need to check for compatibility with the latest releases. In many cases, manufacturers themselves provide open-source libraries to meet consumer demands. This chapter provides a detailed workflow for using Node-RED for industrial dashboard design and CPS modeling.

The Building Blocks of Node-RED

Node-RED is a browser-based programming environment initiated from the command prompt and available for programmers at `http://localhost:1880`. The programming of any module is done with the following Node-RED components:

- Nodes
- Wires
- Flows
- Subflows
- Context
- Workspace

Nodes

The basic flow unit in Node-RED is connected with wires to form consecutive blocks and flows. The flows are realized as SIMD or MIMD to append many nodes in input and output. They are connected as per the programmer's requirements to complete the targeted task. Figure 8-1 shows the formal nodes that are used and connected as MIMD systems with other flows. Once the targeted task is realized as flows with blocks, they can transfer events, messages, and payload to the next consecutive blocks. This event message can be used to configure hardware GPIOs, communication protocols, and timers in many cases.

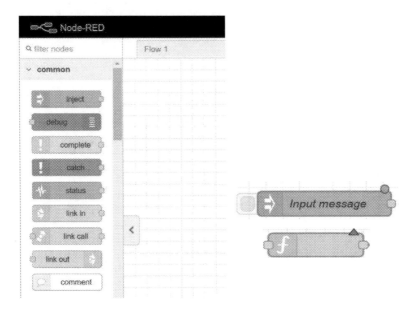

Figure 8-1. *Common nodes, undeployed node, and error node*

The blue cap nodes in the workspace indicate that the node is ready to be deployed, and the red cap in the nodes signifies connection errors. The configuration nodes are special kinds of nodes that are global in context, and the configuration or config is shared by the normal nodes in the flow.

Wire

Figure 8-2 shows how the nodes are connected by a wire. The connection can deliver multiple payload messages to the next consecutive node blocks. The wire is connected by using the left mouse button and dragging from the source node to the destination node. The same process can be done by pressing the Control key and clicking the ports. The new nodes with both ports can be inserted between the wire connecting the two nodes. While doing so, the solid line indicating the wire changes to a dotted line to admit the new node. The one end of the wire can be disconnected and connected with some other node by pressing Shift and clicking the ports. The wire can be deleted by simply selecting it and pressing the Delete key. The wires can be connected between the nodes in one-to-one, one-to-many, many-to-one, and many-to-many fashions based on the purpose and requirements of the task.

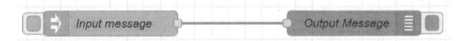

Figure 8-2.   *Wire connecting two nodes*

Flow

The flows are the programs in Node-RED. The tab in the workspace depicts a flow in which a set of nodes is connected through wires. Transferring information from one node to another node in the flow can be done using a payload message. The payload message from the function node can be designed when the node is programmed. The On message tab in the properties dialog box governs the manipulation of payload messages.

Subflow

A subflow is derived as a functional module from the flow. The related operations and the corresponding nodes can be grouped together as a subflow and used whenever required in another flow; the subflow will be part of a submodule that can be added as a single node.

In other words, the subflow is created by packaging the set of nodes into a single node that can be reused. The subflow needs to be added to the palette of nodes before using it in the flow like other nodes in the workspace. Subflows can also be used for reducing the visual complexity of the flow. The detailed implementation can be hidden by using subflows, which can showcase only the essential part of the flow in the workspace if required. The subflows are created using the Create Subflow item in the Subflow menu.

Context

The message passing between the successive nodes is the regular way of transferring messages from one node to another node. But that alone is not sufficient for exchanging information between nodes. The context is like a variable used to exchange data with other nodes. The scope of the context can be at three levels.

- Level 1 is the visibility of the value of the context at the node alone.

- Level 2 is the visibility of the value of the context at the flow so that all the nodes in the flow can access the context.

- Level 3 is global visibility, and the context can be accessed by all the nodes.

Workspace

The workspace is the place where the flows are constructed by dragging nodes from the palettes and connecting the ports of the nodes with wires, as shown in Figure 8-3.

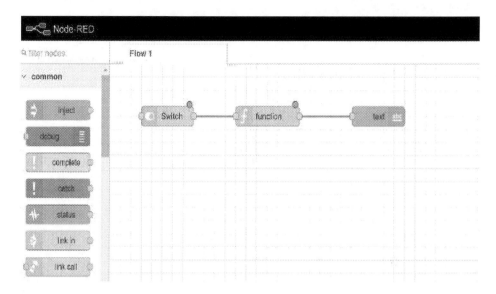

Figure 8-3. *Workspace*

The various flows are arranged in tabs, and switching between flows is as simple as clicking the appropriate tab in the workspace. The workspace as such is very large, and you can open the workspace navigator with the button at the bottom-right corner of the workspace, as shown in Figure 8-4. The visible portion of the workspace in the navigator is shown in the active rectangle, which can be moved in the navigator to any part of the workspace to view the hidden parts of the large flows.

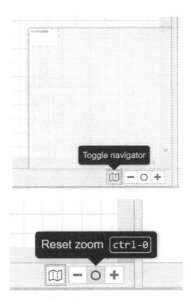

Figure 8-4. *Workspace Navigator and the Zoom tool for workspace*

Sidebar

The sidebar contains several panels that provide various information. The panels are the information panel, help panel, project history panel, debug messages panel, configuration nodes panel, context data panel, and dashboard panel (if the palette contains dashboard nodes), as shown in Figure 8-5.

- The information panel displays the flows, subflows, and global configuration nodes if any.

- The help panel provides the information about Node-RED, nodes in the palette, and functional details of each node when you click any node in the list displayed.

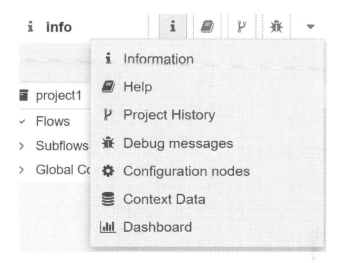

Figure 8-5. *The sidebar panels*

- The project history panel will be available only if the Project menu item is added to the menu, and this panel displays the history of changes that has been carried out on the JSON file.

- The debug messages display the messages received by the debug nodes in the flow along with the date, time, and node name.

- The configuration nodes panel shows the information about the config nodes that are common to all flows involved. The context data panel holds the values of the context if any are used in the flows.

- The dashboard panel displays the layout and theme details of the dashboard where the visual outputs can be viewed.

Writing a Simple Program in Node-RED

The "Hello World" program is familiar to people who do high-level programming, so we will implement a "Hello World" program in Node-RED.

Input Node: Inject

The inject node in Node-RED is for providing input to the system. The input can be of any type such as string, Boolean, number, time, etc. The inject node is available in the palette in the common nodes category, as shown in Figure 8-6. It can be dragged from the palette to the workspace.

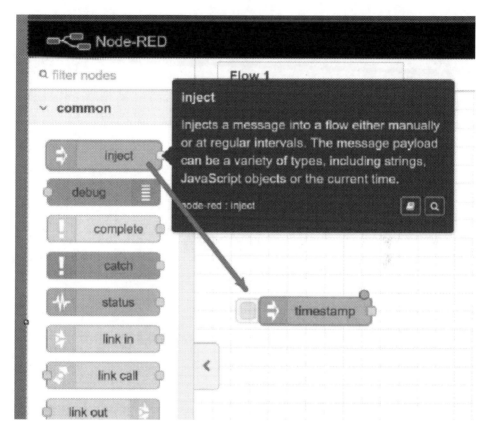

Figure 8-6. *Moving the inject node from palette to workspace*

The notable change at this point is that the moment the inject node is dragged to the workspace, the text displayed on the node changes from "inject" to "timestamp." By default, the node is configured to be time-based triggered. For example, you can set it to repeat an event periodically every minute or so. This can be viewed in the properties dialog box of the inject node. The properties dialog box will be displayed when the node is double-clicked, as shown in Figure 8-7a. It has the name msg.payload for the timestamp setting.

Figure 8-7a. *Properties dialog box of the inject node*

The msg.payload and msg.topic files can be set to the following types: flow, global, string, number, Boolean, json, buffer, timestamp, expression, env variable, and message (as shown in Figure 8-7b).

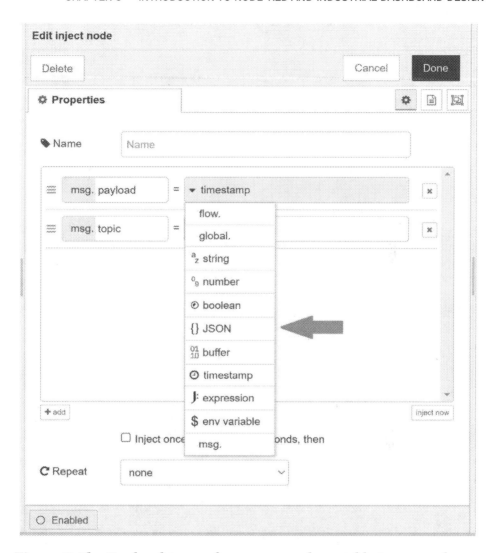

Figure 8-7b. *Payload types of messages exchanged between nodes*

The description of a node can be added in the Description box, as illustrated in Figure 8-7c. The purpose of the node, the set of inputs and its valid values that this node can handle, the node's role in the flow, etc., can be specified in the Description box.

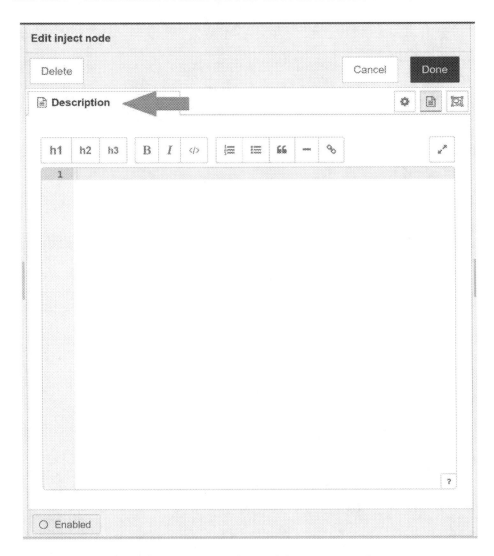

Figure 8-7c. *Description dialog box of the inject node*

The appearance of the node is defined in the Appearance dialog box; the Show check box is selected by default for the node's visibility in the workspace, as shown in Figure 8-7d. The icon style for how the node should be displayed in the workspace can be selected using the drop-down box.

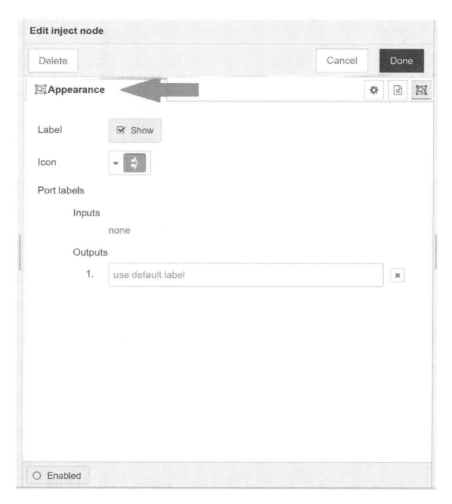

Figure 8-7d. *Appearance dialog box of the inject node*

The output port labels can be specified in the text box given so that the label of the port is displayed when the mouse pointer is moved over the output port of the node in the workspace. Also, the node can be enabled or disabled with the radio button provided in the left corner of the properties dialog box.

In this example, msg.payload is set to the string to display "Hello NodeRed." The name is set to "Input message," as shown in Figure 8-8, in the properties dialog box. The node in the workspace looks like Figure 8-9. The blue circle on the node indicates that it is not yet deployed.

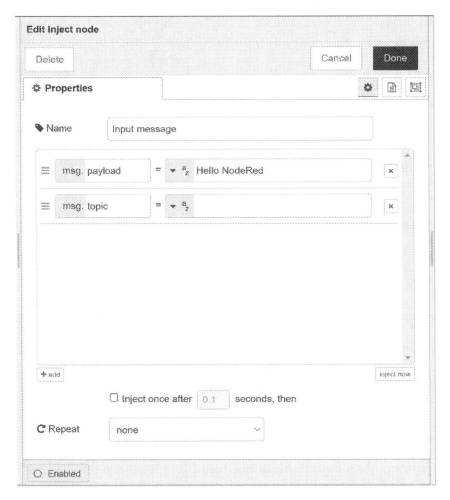

Figure 8-8. *The name and msg.payload setting modified in the properties box*

Figure 8-9. *The inject node after the name is modified*

The debug node is used to display messages in the debug message panel in the sidebar, as shown in Figure 8-10. The messages are received through the input port of the debug node. From the node it is connected through a wire.

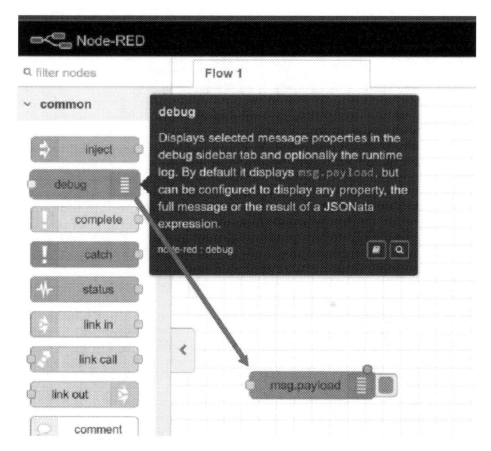

Figure 8-10. *Moving the debug node from the palette to the workspace*

Double-click the debug node in the workspace to display the properties box. The following properties can be set: name, output, and check boxes for the locations to which the messages are transferred or displayed such as debug window, system console, and node status. The output type can be a message (the default), an expression, or a complete message object, as shown in Figure 8-11. As in the inject node, this debug node also has a description and appearance dialog box. The debug panel displays the debug messages along with its date, time, and number of characters in the message.

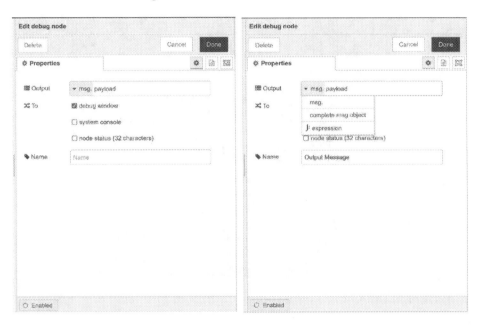

Figure 8-11. *Properties dialog box of the debug node*

The button-like structure at the right end of the debug node can be toggled to deactivate and activate the debug node.

The input node (inject) and the output node (debug) are connected through their output and input ports, respectively. Click the output port of the inject node instance and drag toward the input port of the debug node instance in the workspace. Upon releasing the button, the connection is established between two nodes, as shown in Figure 8-12. The mouse pointer can be moved over the output port of the inject node, and the instance will display the port name updated in its properties dialog box. Similarly, if the mouse pointer is moved over the input port of the debug node, the instance displays the port name updated in its property dialog box. It is good practice to name the ports so they are identifiable. At this stage, the workspace displays two nodes, as shown in Figure 8-13, as undeployed nodes.

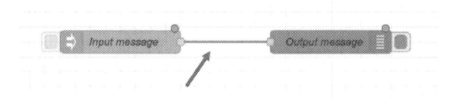

Figure 8-12. *Connecting an instance of the inject node and debug node*

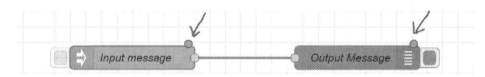

Figure 8-13. *The input message node and output message node in the workspace and undeployed*

The Deployment Processes

The flows are created by organizing the nodes in the workspace and connecting them through wires. In our example flow, the input node and the output node are connected through a wire to illustrate the "Hello World" program in Node-RED. The flow is ready, and it needs to be deployed like the compilation process in other text-based programing languages. The deployment process is simple; just click the Deploy button at the top-right corner, as shown in Figure 8-14. When clicking the Deploy button, check whether the corresponding flow is active on the Workspace tab.

Figure 8-14. *The Deploy button*

After the Deploy button is clicked, a message pops up to indicate it was successfully deployed, as shown in Figure 8-15. The nodes in the workspace display without the blue circle on them, which indicates that they are deployed, as shown in Figure 8-16. Alternatively, if any red triangle appears, it means there is an error that needs to be rectified. The error messages in Node-RED are appropriate and easy to understand and can be resolved quickly in the GUI.

Figure 8-15. *The deployment success message*

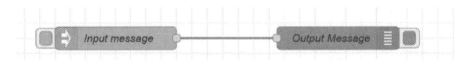

Figure 8-16. *The deployed nodes*

Now, the input message node can be clicked to send a message to the output message node. When clicking the inject node instance, the pop-up message "Successfully injected: input message" will be displayed at the top of the window, as shown in Figure 8-17. Now the debug panel in the sidebar displays the messages as many times as you click the input message node.

Figure 8-17. *Message injected from the inject node instance to the debug node instance*

The message pattern displayed in the debug panel will differ according to the msg.type selection in the property box of the debug node instance. A simple message is displayed with its letter count when the type is message. A message object with id, payload, and topic, along with its values like a key-value pair, will be displayed as shown in Figure 8-18.

Figure 8-18. *The message in the debug panel of the sidebar*

Function

The example program can be extended by adding nodes in between the input and output nodes. The function node can be inserted between the two nodes for any further processing of input and then sent the output message to the debug node. For example, the functions such as string manipulations on the message can be carried out and sent to the debug node. In this example, the function is implemented to change "Hello NodeRed" to "Hello World" or "Welcome NodeRed," and this is sent to the debug node, as shown in Figure 8-19. The properties dialog box of the function shows the code that changes the message to "Welcome NodeRed," as shown in Figure 8-20, and the corresponding debug message in the debug panel.

Figure 8-19. *The function node between input and output*

Figure 8-20. *Properties dialog box of the function and debug message*

User Interface Installation Process

The output of tasks can be viewed as text, but Node-RED is feature rich and supports visual illustrations of outputs through dashboards. The dashboards depict the inferences in terms of gauges, charts, audio, color

pickers, sliders, switches, etc. The dashboard installation happens through
the "Manage palette" submenu, as shown in Figure 8-21. The dialog
box that will appear after opening the Manage palette lists the packages
installed on the Nodes tab, as displayed in Figure 8-22.

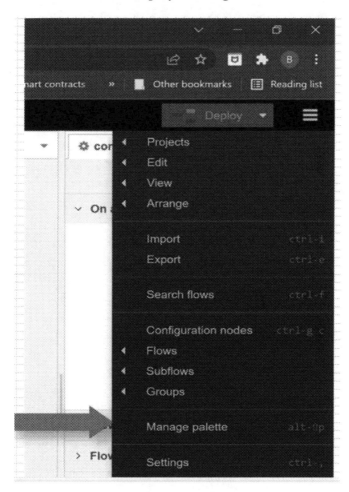

Figure 8-21. *Manage palette submenu*

Figure 8-22. *Nodes tab in the Manage Palette dialog box*

The node packages that are required can be installed using the Install tab. The search box is provided to identify the packages that are available for installation, as depicted in Figure 8-23.

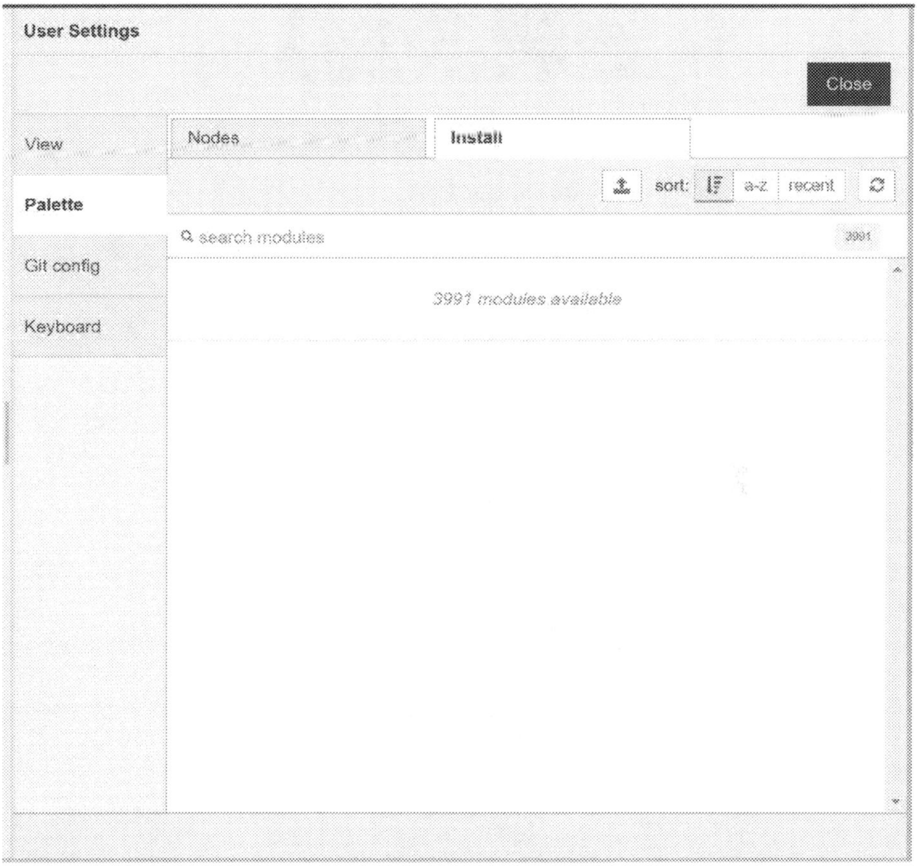

Figure 8-23. *Install tab in the Manage Palette dialog box*

To install the UI, click the Manage palette option and search for *node-red-dashboard* on the Install tab. After installation, Node-RED needs to be restarted to display the UI nodes, as illustrated in Figure 8-24.

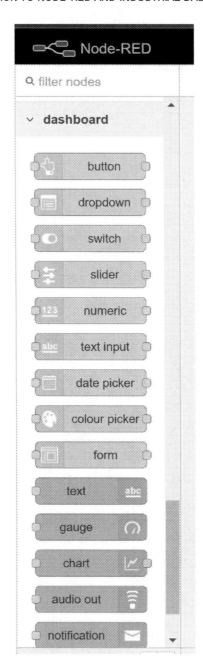

Figure 8-24. *Dashboard nodes*

Dashboard Example

The Node-RED dashboard shows changes in the sensor values in real time. It can have any one of the visualizing components such as a gauge, chart, slider, button, audio, etc.

The CNC machine axis rotation is monitored and reported by Node-RED. The example shown in Figure 8-25 illustrates the monitoring of an accelerometer reading from a CNC machine that is connected through the Message Queueing Telemetry Transport (MQTT) protocol. The protocol is initiated with the appropriate configuration and enables the machine's connectivity with the controller.

The x, y, z data is collected from the machine using the MQTT protocol and transferred to the computer every second. The Node-RED server is executing in the controller computer, which actually monitors the readings of the accelerometer, and if any abnormality is observed in its values, then it will be noted, and the necessary actions are carried out such as sending the control signal to the governing controller that is controlling the rotation.

Figure 8-26 shows the accelerometer output in a graph and a gauge.

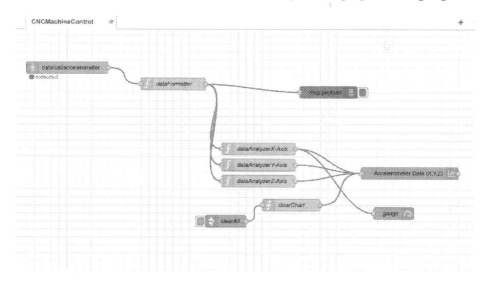

Figure 8-25. *The Node-RED flow for monitoring the accelerometer in the CNC machine*

251

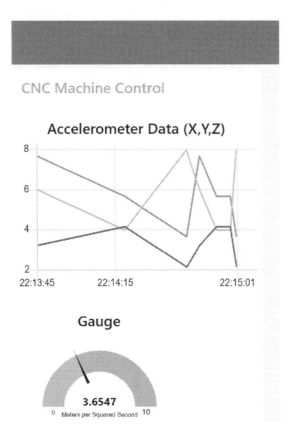

Figure 8-26. *The gauge and graph dashboard for the CNC machine*

Node-RED is a GUI platform to program the desired task.

Summary

This chapter covered Node-RED features and gave appropriate examples. Node-RED helps programmers to develop their own monitoring and control systems that form the basis of CPSs and Industry 4.0.

This chapter also covered the purpose of Node-RED and how flows are developed. It discussed the benefits of Node-RED and its usage for various applications. It covered the fundamental features of Node-RED for the desired library installation. With this knowledge, you can develop your own flows, including libraries, and integrate them with your Node-RED programs. The real-world example showed you how to design and develop industry-based programs to monitor and control real-world systems with a dashboard.

Index

© G.R. Kanagachidambaresan, Bharathi N. 2023
G.R. Kanagachidambaresan and N. Bharathi, *Sensors and Protocols for Industry 4.0*, Maker Innovations Series, https://doi.org/10.1007/978-1-4842-9007-1

T

Printed in the United States
by Baker & Taylor Publisher Services